SANT' ELENA

FOOD
FESTIVALS
OF ITALY

CELEBRATED RECIPES FROM 50 FOOD FAIRS

Leonardo Curti & James O. Fraioli

GIBBS SMITH
ENRICH AND INSPIRE HUMANKIND
Charleston | Santa Fe | Santa Barbara

First Edition

12 11 10 09 08   5 4 3 2 1

Text © 2008 Leonardo Curti and James O. Fraioli
Photographs © 2008 Brian Hodges and Luca Trovato

Published by
Gibbs Smith
P.O. Box 667
Layton, Utah 84041

1-800.835.4993 orders
www.gibbs-smith.com

Designed and produced by Debra McQuiston
Printed and bound in Hong Kong

Library of Congress Cataloging-in-Publication Data

Curti, Leonardo.
 Food festivals of Italy : celebrated recipes from 50 food
fairs / Leonardo Curti and James O. Fraioli. — 1st ed.
    p. cm.
 Includes bibliographical references and index.
 ISBN-13: 978-1-4236-0332-0
 ISBN-10: 1-4236-0332-X
 1. Cookery, Italian. 2. Cookery—Italy. I. Fraioli,
James O., 1968- II. Title.
  TX723.C9478 2007
  641.5945—dc22
                        2008007983

Contents

Buon giorno! For those who don't know us, we are Leonardo Curti and James Fraioli, the Italian chef and Italian author who recently teamed up on the award-winning cookbook *Trattoria Grappolo: Simple Recipes for Traditional Italian Cuisine.*

Trattoria Grappolo, the acclaimed bistro nestled in central California's Wine Country, is a family affair. Inside the kitchen, executive chef and co-proprietor Leonardo Curti labors alongside brothers Alfonso and Giorgio, preparing authentic Italian cuisine with the freshest of local ingredients and fine delicacies from the homeland. Recently featured on Food Network's *Giada's Weekend Getaways* and *The Ellen DeGeneres Show,* reservations at Trattoria Grappolo are a little harder to come by, but it is always worth the wait. The festive but casual bistro atmosphere is the perfect setting to linger with family or friends over a tableful of Trattoria Grappolo favorites such as the almost-too-beautiful-to-eat *Fiori di Zucca Ripieni* (Stuffed Zucchini Blossoms), their irresistible *Involtini di Melanzane* (Rolled Eggplant with Capellini Pasta), the sinfully luscious *Crostata di Mele con Gelato di Vaniglia* (Warm Caramelized Apple Tart with Vanilla Gelato), and the perennial favorite—their traditional Tiramisu.

So when Mr. Gibbs Smith, president of Gibbs Smith, arrived to discuss ideas for our next cookbook, we sat down to talk over a meal at Trattoria Grappolo.

Together we envisioned a book that would honor our Italian homeland—part cookbook and part travelogue, filled with spectacular photographs that would bring the authentic Italian cuisine to life for our readers. Rather than visiting famous restaurants and local bistros, we wanted to take both professional chefs and home cooks on a culinary odyssey of a different sort.

Every year, local regions all across Italy hold special celebrations to honor—and showcase—their most famous local ingredient, dish, or foodstuff. Whether it is celebrating the traditionally aged balsamic vinegar of Modena, fresh buffalo mozzarella from Campania, white truffles dug from the earth in Piemonte, Sicilian couscous, or salami from Tuscany, these food festivals are a chance for the local cooks who know a product the best to vie against each other and take it to its highest culinary potential.

We envisioned a book that would transport both food lovers and travel aficionados to the stall-lined village streets of these local festivals where they would fill their imaginations with the tempting aromas, the warmth of the Italian sun, the spectacular settings, and the easy camaraderie of the friendliest hosts in the world. Each intrepid voyager would then be sent home with a carefully culled collection of the best of each festival's mouthwatering recipes. Before Mr. Smith could finish his Panna Cotta drizzled with caramel, *Food Festivals of Italy: Celebrated Recipes from 50 Food Fairs* was born.

With travel photographer *par excellence* Brian Hodges, renowned food photographer Luca Trovato, and the incomparable food stylist Rori Trovato, we set off to explore, experience, and bring home to you a sampling of Italian food festivals and their delectable treats. These festivals come in all sizes, colors, and shapes. Some are intimate afternoon affairs that seem to suddenly spring to life along a lava-cobbled street or behind a café or local church. Our favorites of these smaller festivals include the Chile Pepper Festival in Calabria and the Veneto Bean Festival, which is set against the jaw-dropping backdrop of the white Dolomite Mountains.

Some festivals are extravagant, gala affairs that draw thousands of gourmands from across the globe. Several have grown so popular they literally take over a town, becoming the headline attraction for a region and putting the

Italian cooking is among the richest and most varied anywhere

with dishes perfect for every occasion, from the quick late night snack, to weekend get-togethers.

We'd swear we could not take another bite, **then found ourselves reaching for a fire-roasted chestnut from a local grower, sampling succulent pork served with cornmeal porridge, or gratefully accepting one more slice of handcrafted salami infused with Barolo wine and black truffles.**

local village—and its delectable regional specialties—on the world's culinary map. One such favorite of locals and visitors is the Pizza Fest in Campania, others are the National Truffle Festivals in Liguria and Piemonte, and the Chocolate Festival in Umbria. In large festivals like these, we found throngs of residents and tourists strolling together through the streets, sipping wine, and nibbling on local food specialties, while medieval-costumed performers amused the children, and enchanting music wafted through the air. The smells of barbecue would fill the streets of one festival, the rich aroma of chocolate another, and the pungent scent of cheese a third. We'd swear we could not take another bite, then found ourselves reaching for a fire-roasted chestnut from a local grower, sampling succulent pork served with cornmeal porridge, or gratefully accepting one more slice of handcrafted salami infused with Barolo wine and black truffles.

We have yet to find anyone who believes us, but it was truly hard, demanding work to uncover, taste, and talk the purveyors out of the most prized recipes at these various food festivals. Our labors continued when we returned home and had to select the top one hundred of all we had collected, paying close attention to originality and sim-

plicity, and to those that exemplify traditional home-style Italian cooking. Some of our all-time favorites include *Spiedino di Scamorza* (smoked mozzarella grilled with crisp pancetta), *Bocconcini di Salame e Cipolla* (Italian salami slices folded over crisp scallions served with dollops of creamy mascarpone cheese), *Insalata di Fragole e Parmigiano-Reggiano* (luscious strawberries ripened by the sun and split and stuffed with wedges of Parmigiano-Reggiano), *Cotelette di Rana* (tender golden-fried frog legs fanned on a bed of arugula leaves), *Coniglio al Vino Bianco* (oven-roasted rabbit with aromatic herbs and white wine), *Soufflé di Fichi d'India* (an Italian handcrafted soufflé filled with sweet prickly pear), and *Sorbetto al Limone* (a refreshing lemon sorbet served in frozen lemon shells).

Accompanying these recipes are extraordinary photographs showcasing the food, the festivals, and some of the people who make them so special. Thanks to the tireless efforts and uncompromising artistry of our photography crew, we were able to capture the heart and soul of extraordinary dishes and bring them home to share with you. A few festivals we were unfortunately unable to attend and must—like you—savor in our imaginations; we have done our best to bring you the culinary feel of these festivals with help from

Valle d' Aosta

Piemonte

Lombardia

Trentino Alto Adige

Veneto

Friuli-Venezia Guilia

Liguria

Emilia Romagna

Toscana

Marche

Umbria

Abruzzo

Lazio

Molise

Campania

Basilicata

Puglia

Sardegna

Calabria

Sicilia

N
nw · ne
W · E
sw · se
S

The 20 distinct regions that shape Italy also serve as the birthplaces of spirited food festivals, many of which appear in the exciting pages ahead. While perusing the festivals, refer to this map to locate where you are.

The Italian piazza is the center of public life, where cafés, restaurants, markets, and

celebrated food festivals welcome locals and visitors alike

the Italian Government Tourist Board and other research. But unlike American festivals with their full-featured Web sites, teams of festival administrators, and toll-free numbers to call for more information, many Italian food festivals are still intensely local. If you are passionate to learn more than what we have been able to provide, or would like to explore the long list of Italian food festivals yourself, we highly recommend booking a flight, renting (or hiring) a car, and allowing yourself plenty of time to scout out, discover, and savor what is often not advertised. Not only will you come away with a deeper love for authentic Italian cuisine—and perhaps a collection of your own special recipes—but you will meet some of the most gracious, unpretentious, friendly people, justifiably proud of their heritage and of the Italian foods their families have prepared for centuries.

In this book, there is nothing that you cannot make at home. Even if an ingredient is not stocked in your local grocery, the Internet and overnight airfreight have shrunk the globe and you can have almost any ingredient delivered right to your front doorstep. But do take the time to select the freshest ingredients possible, indulge yourself and your guests by choosing a special bowl or platter for presentation, and don't, in the rush to the table, overlook the final garnish or drizzle of olive oil before offering up the fruits of your labor. Believe us, these little things do make a difference.

We hope you receive great pleasure from the recipes in this book and will share them with your family and friends; may you also someday find yourself strolling down a festival-crowded street in some small Italian village, trying hard to finish a refreshing gelato before it melts in the afternoon sun. Until then, enjoy the tantalizing photographs and tastes from Italy's finest food festivals.

Buon Appetito!

Chef Leonardo Curti & James O. Fraioli

PART ONE: *Antipasti*

ARTICHOKE FESTIVAL 24
Guazzetto di Carciofi *artichoke and potato stew*
Carciofi Ripieni *stuffed Italian artichokes*

BALSAMIC VINEGAR FESTIVAL 26
Scaglie con Parmigiano *parmesan wedges drizzled with aged balsamic vinegar*
Zuppa di Porri e Patate con Balsamico *potato and leek soup with aged balsamic vinegar*

CHILE PEPPER FESTIVAL 30
Frittelle di Bianchetti *Italian fish cakes*
Crema di Peperoncino *peperoncino spread*

COUSCOUS FEST 38
Couscous Mediterraneo *Mediterranean couscous*
Couscous di Pesce *seafood couscous*

FOCACCIA FESTIVAL 40
Focaccia al Forno *fresh baked focaccia*

GARLIC FESTIVAL 44
Crema di Pomodoro con Aglio *tomato basil garlic bisque*
Crostino con Aglio *toasted bread with garlic*

GOAT CHEESE FESTIVAL 46
Tortino di Formaggio Caprino *handcrafted goat cheese cakes*
Insalata di Bietole Gherigli e Formaggio Caprino *roasted beet and goat cheese salad*

GRAPE FESTIVAL 50
Spiedini di Formaggi e Uva Nera *black grape and fontina cheese skewers*
Mousse di Granchio con Uva *crab mousse topped with white grapes*

MOZZARELLA FESTIVAL 54
Mozzarella Impanata *fried Italian buffalo mozzarella*
Spiedino di Scamorza *smoked mozzarella with crisp pancetta*

NATIONAL WHITE TRUFFLE FAIR 62
Tagliatelle al Tartufo Bianco *tagliatelle pasta with white truffles*
Carpaccio di Bue al Tartufo Bianco *beef carpaccio with white truffles*
Risotto al Profumo di Tartufo Bianco *white truffle risotto*
Crostini al Tartufo *truffle crostini*

PARMESAN CHEESE FESTIVAL 70
Insalata di Fragole e Parmigiano-Reggiano *Parmigiano-Reggiano strawberry salad*
Fonduta al Parmigiano *Parmigiano-Reggiano fondue*

PROSCIUTTO FESTIVAL 76
Prosciutto con Melone *fresh cantaloupe with sliced prosciutto*
Asparagi al Prosciutto *asparagus wrapped in prosciutto*

SALAMI FESTIVAL 80
Bocconcini di Salame e Cipolla *Italian salami with green onions and mascarpone cheese*
Piadina con Salame *Italian salami flatbread sandwich*

SNAIL FESTIVAL 88
Lumache al Gorgonzola Dolce *snails with sweet gorgonzola*
Lumache con Basilico *snails tossed with pesto*

TRADITIONAL CHESTNUT HUNT 92
Frittata di Castagne *chestnut omelet*
Zuppa di Castagne con Porcini *chestnut and porcini mushroom soup*

ARTICHOKE FESTIVAL, MARCHE

MARCHE IS A COMPLEX, COMPOSITE TERRITORY, where the history, culture, and landscape have combined to create an extraordinary and unique place. From the Apennine Mountains to seaside villages, from deep green valleys to flatlands, the region has gradually taken to organic farming to raise the wide range of food products used in their centuries-old dishes. One such crop that does extraordinarily well in Marche is the artichoke. The renowned Marchigiano artichokes, along with Monteluponese artichokes, are the star attractions at the annual Sagra del Carciofo, or Artichoke Festival—a much anticipated festival showcasing all things artichoke at numerous food stalls and dinners held in the town square.

GUAZZETTO DI CARCIOFI
artichoke and potato stew

SERVES 4

4 tablespoons extra virgin olive oil, plus more for garnish

3 garlic cloves

3 cups water

Salt and pepper, to taste

4 artichokes, peeled, choked, removed and halved

1 bay leaf

2 medium Yukon gold potatoes, skinned and cut into large cubes

Freshly grated Parmesan cheese

1 tablespoon freshly chopped Italian parsley

In a sauté pan over medium-high heat, add the olive oil and garlic and sauté until garlic is soft and golden.

Add the water, salt, pepper, artichokes, bay leaf, and potatoes. Cover and cook over low heat for 20 minutes, or until artichokes are tender.

Transfer to individual serving bowls and drizzle each with olive oil and sprinkle with Parmesan cheese. Top with some Italian parsley and serve with toasted slices of country bread.

CARCIOFI RIPIENI

stuffed Italian artichokes

SERVES 4

4 medium artichokes
4 cups water
1 ripe lemon, halved
1/4 cup olive oil, plus more as needed
2 tablespoons freshly chopped Italian parsley
4 cloves garlic, minced
1 1/2 cups Italian breadcrumbs
1 tablespoon capers, drained and chopped
1/4 cup freshly grated Pecorino-Romano cheese
2 eggs
1 cup water
1/2 cup white wine
Salt and pepper, to taste

Clean the artichokes and remove the outer leaves. With a sharp knife, remove the tops and stems. Using your fingers, open the artichokes carefully. Remove the "hair" and the innermost leaves, exposing the choke. Place each artichoke in a bowl filled with 4 cups water and the juice from both lemon halves to prevent chokes from turning black.

In a large bowl, mix 4 tablespoons olive oil, parsley, garlic, breadcrumbs and capers. Add the cheese and eggs and stir to incorporate.

Remove the artichokes from the water and pat dry. In a piping bag, or by hand, stuff the artichokes with the breadcrumb mixture.

In a sauté pan over medium heat, arrange the stuffed artichokes tightly so they are all standing up. Add 1 cup water, white wine, salt, and pepper; drizzle tops of the artichokes with olive oil. Allow to simmer in the pan, half covered with a lid, until liquid is almost evaporated, about 25 minutes, or until chokes are tender.

NOTE: Add more water if the liquid evaporates before the chokes are finished cooking. Serve warm or chilled, with a drizzle of extra virgin olive oil.

BALSAMIC VINEGAR FESTIVAL, EMILIA ROMAGNA

"EMILIA ROMAGNA" — say it aloud and even the syllables roll on the tongue like a rich morsel of cheese or sip of fine wine. This is a region with an incredible wealth and diversity of ingredients raised to a peak of perfection that seems impossible elsewhere. As one might expect, Emilia Romagna is home to many festivals celebrating its cuisine, but there is one so popular that entire tourist packages are arranged around it: the Balsamica Festival in Modena. The balsamic vinegar of Modena is no ordinary vinegar. Its depth, complexity, and fusion of flavors make it an extraordinary addition to everything from vanilla gelato, to bite-size wedges of Parmigiano-Reggiano, to a radicchio salad. True Modena balsamic vinegar takes so long to develop that mothers include small barrels in their daughter's dowries. The famous Balsamica festival explores the history, creation, and uses of this unique product with exhibitions, tastings, food and wine events, guided tours of the vinegar-making plants, courses and seminars on cooking with vinegar, and parties in the town squares where special meals based on the traditional balsamic vinegar are served.

SCAGLIE CON PARMIGIANO
Parmesan wedges drizzled with aged balsamic vinegar

SERVES 4

1 pound Parmesan cheese, cut into large chunks
Traditional balsamic vinegar (preferably aged 25 to 30 years)

On a serving platter, scatter bite-size wedges of Parmesan. Drizzle each piece with the balsamic vinegar. Serve at room temperature.

ZUPPA DI PORRI E PATATE CON BALSAMICO

potato and leek soup with aged balsamic vinegar

SERVES 4–6

1 onion

1 carrot

1 stalk celery

1 clove garlic

1 sprig rosemary

1 small handful sage leaves

3½ ounces bacon, finely chopped

Salt and pepper, to taste

Olive oil, as needed

3½ tablespoons butter

1 cup dry white wine

2 pounds fresh leeks, sliced in thin strips

1½ pounds potatoes, peeled and cut into small cubes

1 bay leaf

4 cups chicken stock

2 teaspoons traditional balsamic vinegar (preferably aged 25 to 30 years), as needed

Finely chop the first six ingredients. Cook bacon until crispy. Crumble and set aside.

In a sauté pan over medium heat, add the salt, pepper, olive oil, and butter and slowly sauté the chopped vegetables.

Add the wine, leeks, potatoes, and bay leaf. Add the chicken stock and cover. Lower the heat and let simmer until the vegetables are cooked; remove from heat. Puree in a blender until creamy. Add more stock if soup appears dry.

Transfer soup to individual bowls and top with the crispy bacon and a drizzle of balsamic vinegar.

Traditional balsamic vinegar is like

Italy's fine wines—perfectly aged with a cornucopia of flavors.

CHILE PEPPER FESTIVAL, CALABRIA

THE SPICY HEAT OF chile peppers is well known for bringing a quick burst of flavor to a dish. However, when cooked long and slow, both fresh and dried chiles can produce layer upon layer of deep, rich flavors which can come from no other ingredient. The cooks of Calabria are masters of both the short and long uses of chiles. It is a rare Calabrian household that does not have a colorful string of chile peppers hanging out a door or window, and most families grow their own chiles at home in the garden or in a fanciful pot. Many of the best-known Calabrian dishes keep the cook busy for hours, following jealously guarded traditional recipes that seem as much ritual as technique. Other dishes are plain and simple. But all are extremely healthy and feature strong, distinctive flavors. The region's fascination with chiles comes to a crescendo at the annual Chile Pepper Festival, where dish after dish is flavored with chiles: long or round chiles; red, orange, yellow or green chiles; fresh, dried, or crushed chiles. It is the festival for the spice lover and not the faint of heart.

FRITTELLE DI BIANCHETTI
Italian fish cakes

SERVES 4

1 pound fresh bianchetti (or fresh anchovy or white fish), cooked and crumbled into fine pieces

3 eggs

1/2 cup milk

2 tablespoons flour

1 tablespoon freshly grated Parmesan cheese

Salt and pepper, to taste

1 tablespoon Italian peperoncino powder

2 cloves garlic, diced

1 tablespoon freshly chopped Italian parsley

1/2 cup olive oil

In a bowl, mix the bianchetti, eggs, milk, flour, Parmesan cheese, salt, pepper, peperoncino powder, garlic, and parsley.

In a nonstick pan over medium-high heat, add the olive oil. When ready, spoon a dollop of the bianchetti mixture into the pan and cook each side until golden brown. Serve immediately.

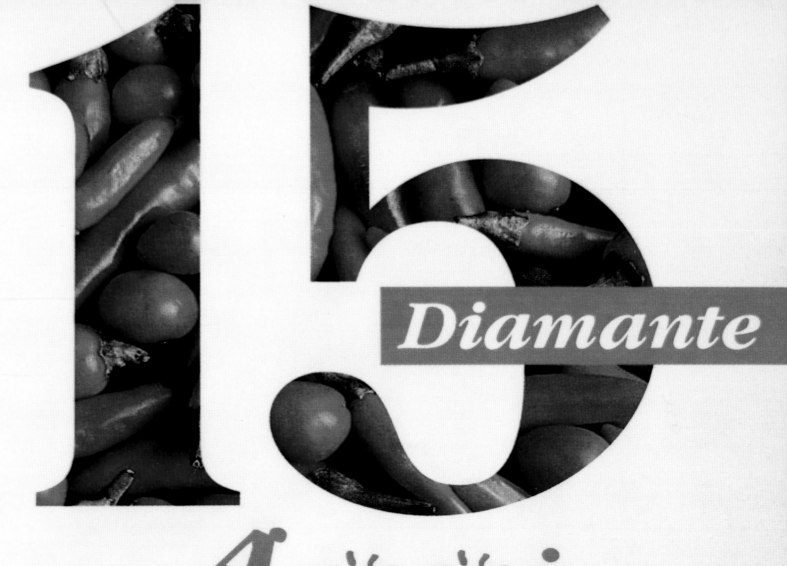

15

Diamante

Anni
tutti
piccanti

Quindicesimo Festival
del Peperoncino
Diamante 5-9 settembre

Chile peppers are capsicums, in the same family as bell

peppers and paprika pods. They range in flavor from rich and sweet, to fiery hot.

Dried as a spice, enjoyed raw, or infused in olive oil, Italian peppers

add a **flavorful kick** and exquisite color.

CREMA DI PEPERONCINO
peperoncino spread

MAKES 1 CUP

1 tablespoon coriander seeds
4 cloves garlic
40 fresh Italian peperoncino peppers
8 tablespoons extra virgin olive oil
1 tablespoon salt

Using a mortar and pestle or blender, grind the coriander seeds and garlic cloves.

In a steamer or sauté pan with a little water, steam the peppers for about 10 minutes, or until tender. Remove from heat and let cool.

Add the peperoncino peppers a small batch at a time to the garlic mixture and grind until pasty. Add the olive oil and salt and continue to grind until well incorporated.

Serve the pepper mixture atop freshly toasted bread.

NOTE: Italian peperoncino peppers are red in color and extremely hot; they are not the pale-green peperoncinos commonly served in the United States under the same name.

ℭOUSCOUS FEST, SICILIA

IT IS CALLED "THE FOOD OF PEACE," and once a year, men and women from four continents, who share a passion for cooking, gather to celebrate on a very special island off the toe of Italy's boot. The food is couscous; the island is Sicily—a place of forbidding rocky cliffs to the north; low, sandy beaches to the south; and sky so blue, water so clear, and sun so bright that in ancient myths it was known as the paradise of the Mediterranean Sea. Sicily's land and sea are generous with delectable ingredients, from fish to meat, from vegetables to citrus, as well as grapes, pistachios, and almonds. Couscous—fine granules of semolina wheat rolled and shaped and then coated with finely ground wheat flour—is the perfect backdrop for the diverse flavors of the island's rich cornucopia.

COUSCOUS MEDITERRANEO
Mediterranean couscous

SERVES 4

4 cups water
2 tablespoons olive oil
1 tablespoon sea salt
2 cups uncooked couscous, unseasoned
1 cup diced Roma tomatoes
1/4 cup diced red onion
1/2 cup diced cucumber
2 tablespoons red wine vinegar
1/4 cup olive oil
Salt and pepper, to taste
Fresh basil leaves, for garnish

Bring the water to a boil in a saucepan. Add 2 tablespoons olive oil and the sea salt; remove from heat. Add the couscous, stirring quickly. Cover the saucepan immediately. Let stand for 3 to 4 minutes and fluff with a fork.

Add the tomatoes, onion, cucumber, red wine vinegar, olive oil, salt, and pepper. Fluff together with a fork and garnish with fresh basil leaves. Serve immediately.

Couscous di Pesce

seafood couscous

SERVES 4

1/3 cup extra virgin olive oil
1 medium yellow onion, sliced
4 cloves garlic, whole
1 pound black mussels
1 pound manila clams
1 pound calamari, sliced into rings
1 pound halibut, cut into 4 pieces
1 pound salmon, cut into 4 pieces
4 basil leaves
Salt and pepper, to taste
1/4 cup white wine
Pinch of crushed red pepper
1 tablespoon oregano
1 cup chopped canned tomato
4 cups clam juice
1 pound large shrimp or prawns, in shell
1 1/2 cups uncooked couscous
1 tablespoon freshly chopped Italian parsley
Lemon wedges

In a large stockpot over high heat, add the olive oil, onion, and garlic and cook for about 5 minutes or until onion and garlic are soft and golden.

Add all of the seafood except the shrimp.

Add the basil. Cook for about 4 minutes and add the salt, pepper, wine, crushed red pepper, and oregano. Cook for another 2 minutes. Add the tomatoes and clam juice. Reduce to medium heat, cover pot and cook for about 20 minutes, or until all the fish is tender and flaky.

Add the shrimp several minutes before cooking is complete.

Remove pot from heat and add couscous. Let stand for 3 to 4 minutes and fluff with a fork.

NOTE: There should be ample liquid so the couscous can cook. If not, add additional clam juice and wine in small amounts.

Divide portions into four deep bowls. Top with parsley and serve with a slice of country bread and a wedge of lemon.

FOCACCIA FESTIVAL, LIGURIA

LIGURIA IS THE NAME of the region situated between Tuscany and Provence. Graced with 220 miles of coastline and ringed by mountains, the region's sweet-smelling breezes carry the life-affirming scents of the sea, herbs, flowers, and pine trees. But Liguria's salty air and humidity make it difficult to bake bread and keep it from spoiling. As has happened so many times throughout the Italian peninsula, local cooks met adversity with ingenuity and, some time in the Middle Ages, created the food of the Ligurian people: focaccia. Devised to be eaten hot out of the oven, plain or topped with scattered onions and olives, left to its own rich aroma or infused with rosemary, focaccia can be simple and humble on an evocative palate, inspiring the most sophisticated culinary combinations. When the Focaccia Festival fills the town streets, the region's best cooks showcase focaccias paired beautifully with all things Ligurian, from its delicate mountain herbs to the freshest edibles of the sea pounding its shores.

FOCACCIA AL FORNO
fresh baked focaccia

MAKES 2 LOAVES

1 package (1.5 ounces) dry active yeast
1½ cups lukewarm water
½ cup extra virgin olive oil, plus more
2 pounds flour
½ tablespoon salt
Sea salt to taste

Dissolve the yeast in lukewarm water until foamy; add the olive oil to the mixture.

Sift flour and salt together into a stand mixer with a dough hook attached. Turn on low speed and add the yeast mixture. Work the dough for about 15 minutes to obtain a smooth, elastic dough.

Divide the dough into two pieces and then place individually into oiled bowls; cover with plastic wrap and set aside, allowing the doughs to double in size.

After the dough has risen, remove from bowls and work by stretching each dough into a shallow baking pan and punch down with fingertips. Sprinkle with sea salt and drizzle with olive oil over top. Allow the doughs to rise half of their size.

Preheat the oven to 400 degrees F. Place both dough pans into oven and bake for about 1 hour, or until golden brown.

NOTE: For an even tastier focaccia, sprinkle finely grated Parmesan cheese, sliced olives, or sliced red onions over top before baking.

Italy's rustic artisan breads are best

enjoyed hot from the oven with a sprinkle of sea salt and extra virgin olive oil.

GARLIC FESTIVAL, EMILIA ROMAGNA

GARLIC HAS BEEN WORSHIPPED by the ancient Egyptians, chewed by Greek Olympian athletes, and for centuries—according to some—kept vampires at bay. From the earliest of times, garlic has also had a unique role in food. Raw, it has a hot, biting taste; but when cooked it mellows into a sweet, rich, binding flavor that today is almost synonymous with Italian cuisine. In fact, one would be hard pressed to find an Italian kitchen that does not have a bulb of garlic, or more likely an entire string of them, dangling somewhere in a window or cupboard or gracing a counter or cutting board. At the Garlic Festival in Emilia Romagna, garlic is king. Brave visitors can taste the differences among an incredible variety of raw garlic, while everyone can enjoy sampling dishes where the pungent bulb has slipped into the background medley of flavors to transform savory meals into extraordinary culinary experiences.

CREMA DI POMODORO CON AGLIO
tomato basil garlic bisque

SERVES 4–6

2 tablespoons olive oil
3 tablespoons unsalted butter
1 large onion, diced
1¹/₂ tablespoons minced fresh garlic
Salt and pepper, to taste
¹/₂ teaspoon thyme leaves
3 tablespoons chopped fresh basil
2 cups Italian plum tomatoes or 1 (2-pound)
can whole peeled or fresh tomatoes
4 cups chicken broth, divided
¹/₂ cup flour

In a sauté pan over medium-high heat, add the olive oil and butter. Cook the onion until wilted but not brown. Add the garlic and cook until tender. Do not brown or burn the garlic or butter. Add the salt, pepper, herbs, tomatoes, and 3 1/2 cups chicken broth; simmer for about 20 minutes.

Make a roux with the remaining chicken broth, adding the flour to thicken. (**NOTE:** Add more flour if roux is too thin.) Add the roux to the soup. Then purée soup in a blender. Return to heat and cook about 15 minutes longer. Serve with fresh country bread.

CROSTINO CON AGLIO
toasted bread with garlic

SERVES 4

4 slices country-style bread (or ciabatta)
4 cloves garlic
¹/₄ cup extra virgin olive oil
Sea salt to taste

Grill bread slices until toasted on each side. Rub one whole clove of garlic on each slice of bread.

Drizzle the bread with olive oil and sprinkle with sea salt.

GOAT CHEESE FESTIVAL, LAZIO

IN THE HEART OF the Lazio region lies Rome, the Eternal City, home to breathtaking architecture, centuries of artistic wonders, and a diverse, cosmopolitan population. Although the lure of urban Rome can be overpowering, the surrounding Lazio region offers extraordinary opportunities: expansive beaches, pine woods, rugged mountain peaks, rolling hills, volcanoes, and vast plains. Add historical treasures like Etruscan ruins and monasteries built by St. Francis and it is easy to understand why thousands of visitors flock to this picture-postcard region every year. The cuisine of Lazio reflects its stunning beauty and diversity but also the straight-forward common sense of the shepherds and farmers of the land. Select the freshest local ingredients at the peak of the season and prepare them simply. One favorite dish is tender, milk-fed lamb, usually baked and served with seasonal vegetables. Another is Marzolina—a unique goat cheese made in the mountains of the Monti Aurunci Natural Park. Tradition demands that Marzolina be left to mature for several days on wooden racks and then be transferred to glass jars to age for an additional several months to perfect its distinctive flavor. The Marzoline Festival is the time when all the cheese makers of the region showcase the best of their homegrown goat cheeses—make your way to Lazio, and enjoy!

TORTINO DI FORMAGGIO CAPRINO
handcrafted goat cheese cakes

SERVES 4

1 pound fresh goat cheese
Salt and pepper, to taste
2 eggs, whisked
4 cups Italian breadcrumbs
1/2 cup olive oil
Homemade Tomato Sauce (see page 116)

Divide and form the goat cheese into four equal cakes and then sprinkle with salt and pepper. Dip each cheese cake into the beaten eggs and then into the breadcrumbs. Repeat so each cake is double dipped in the egg and breadcrumbs; set aside.

Pour the olive oil into a sauté pan over high heat and add the goat cheese cakes. Fry until golden brown on each side. Serve immediately with Fresh Tomato Sauce on the side.

INSALATA DI BIETOLE GHERIGLI E FORMAGGIO CAPRINO
roasted beet and goat cheese salad

SERVES 4

2 beets
1/2 pound mixed field greens
Salt and pepper, to taste
1/4 cup olive oil
4 tablespoons balsamic vinegar
1/2 cup crumbled fresh goat cheese
1/4 cup ground walnuts

Wash and dry the beets. Wrap in foil and place on a baking sheet. Bake for about 20 minutes in a preheated 375-degree F oven. When finished, remove the beets and let cool. When cool, peel and slice the beets paper-thin.

On a large serving plate, layer the beet slices.

Toss the greens with the salt, pepper, olive oil, and balsamic vinegar until well incorporated.

Mound the salad in the middle of plate over the beets and top with goat cheese and walnuts.

GRAPE FESTIVAL, TRENTINO

VISITORS TO THE NORTHERN ITALIAN region of Trentino-Alto Adige will immediately notice the Germanic influence of neighboring Austria. But they will also find the same warm hospitality and charm of Italy's other distinctive regions, and those who explore Trentino's countryside will discover the gastronomic "essences" of the region: orchard-grown fruits, farm-fresh vegetables, and what is perhaps Trentino's most famous product—grapes. Spectacular grapes mean great wines, of course, but at Trentino's annual Grape Festival, the grapes themselves share the stage, as well as the other diverse bounty from the region's gardens and orchards. One cannot spend a better afternoon than wandering the stalls, sampling delicious local specialties expertly paired with some of Italy's finest wines, all set against the Dolomite Mountains.

SPIEDINI DI FORMAGGI E UVA NERA
black grape and fontina cheese skewers

SERVES 4

1/2 pound black grapes
12 ounces fontina cheese, cubed
1/4 cup orange blossom honey

On four skewers, alternate the grapes and cubed cheese.

Plate the skewers and drizzle with the orange blossom honey. Serve slightly chilled.

MOUSSE DI GRANCHIO CON UVA
crab mousse topped with white grapes

SERVES 4

1 pound fresh picked crabmeat, precooked
2 tablespoons freshly grated Parmesan cheese
1/2 tablespoon lemon juice
Salt to taste
Dash of cayenne pepper
1/2 cup heavy cream, whipped to soft peaks
2 egg whites, whipped to soft peaks
1 bunch white grapes, individually sliced

In a bowl, mix the crabmeat, Parmesan cheese, lemon juice, salt, and cayenne pepper. Fold in the cream and then the egg whites.

Meanwhile, wet four 6-ounce ramekins with water and divide the mixture in the ramekins. Refrigerate for about 2 hours. Top with the sliced grapes and serve chilled.

The charmed land of Tuscany

is synonymous with remarkable wines, most notably Chianti

MOZZARELLA FESTIVAL, CAMPANIA

CAMPANIA IS A CAPTIVATING land, filled with Italian gardens, mosaics and wall paintings, museums, and archaeological treasures, such as the ancient lost cities of Pompeii and Herculaneum.

The famous writer Cervantes, who penned *Don Quixote*, remarked that Campania is the most beautiful place he ever visited. Equally captivating are the food specialties of the region such as its exceptional pastas and extra virgin olive oil. Particularly sought after is Campania's inimitable mozzarella, made from the milk of Campania buffaloes. The cheese takes its name from the part of the production cycle when the curd, after being stretched, is *mozzata* (an Italian term meaning "lopped off") to obtain pieces of desired size. Visitors to the popular Festival of Mozzarella Buffalo Cheese can go behind the scenes and witness the production cycle, as well as taste a seemingly infinite variety of uses for this celebrated cheese.

MOZZARELLA IMPANATA
fried Italian buffalo mozzarella

SERVES 4

1 pound (2 or 3 balls) mozzarella di bufala, drained
1 cup flour
2 eggs
Pinch of salt
1 cup Italian breadcrumbs
Olive oil for frying

ROASTED BELL PEPPER SAUCE

2 red bell peppers, roasted and chopped
1/2 cup sliced white onion
1 1/2 cups cream
Salt and pepper, to taste
2 fresh basil leaves, chopped

Slice the mozzarella in half, or in 1/2-inch-thick slices for smaller pieces.

Place the flour in a bowl; set aside. Whisk the eggs in a bowl with salt; set aside. Place breadcrumbs in a bowl; set aside.

In a frying pan with 1 inch of olive oil, heat over medium-high. Take the slices of mozzarella and dust each one with flour, then dip in the egg and then the breadcrumbs. Now double coat each piece by re-dipping in the egg and then the breadcrumbs. Continue this process for the remaining slices. Place each slice in the hot oil and fry until breadcrumbs are golden on each side. Remove from oil and let rest on a plate lined with paper towels. Serve with the Roasted Bell Pepper Sauce.

For the sauce, sauté the bell peppers and onion in a saucepan for 4 minutes over medium heat. Add the cream, salt, pepper, and basil leaves and continue to cook for 5 minutes more. Remove from heat and pour into a blender. Purée and strain.

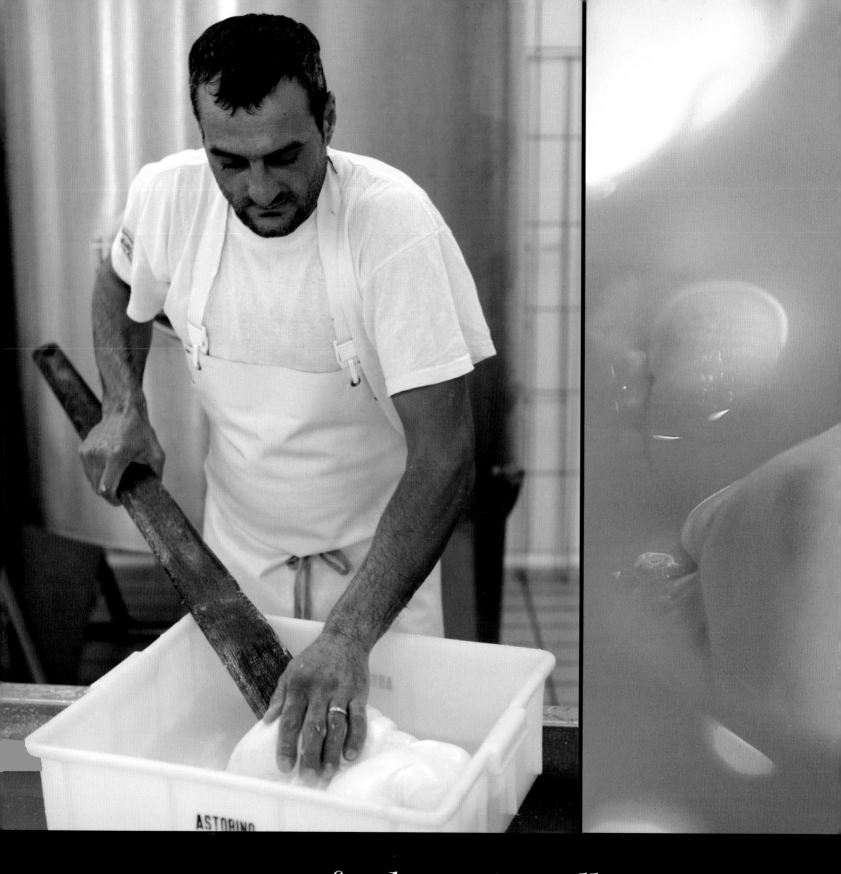

Creamy goat cheese and fresh mozzarella are just two authentic

Italian cheeses—indispensable ingredients featured in many wonderful dishes.

Spiedino di Scamorza
smoked mozzarella with crisp pancetta

SERVES 4

16 slices pancetta, thinly sliced
1 pound smoked mozzarella, cut
into 1-inch cubes
Fresh arugula or field greens

Wrap 1 or 2 slices pancetta around each cube of cheese.

Add 3 or 4 pancetta-wrapped smoked mozzarella cubes to four skewers.

Over a hot grill, cook the cubes, rotating often, until the pancetta is brown and crisp, and the cheese is partially melted.

When finished, plate one skewer per serving and garnish with fresh arugula or field greens. Serve immediately.

Insalata Caprese is the perfect combination of creamy Mozzarella di Bufala Campania, extra virgin

olive oil, fresh basil, and **sun-ripened tomatoes** bursting with flavor.

National White Truffle Fair, Piemonte

FROM HARSH PEAKS, to the charming and romantic atmosphere of the lakes, through the hills between the Alps and the great Po Valley, a visit to Piemonte (meaning "the foot of the mountains") is an exploration that yields new discoveries with every turn in the path. How fitting that one of the world's most highly prized culinary treasures—and one of its hardest to find—is a Piemonte specialty: the truffle. At the National White Truffle Fair, envious visitors can listen to a *trifulau*, or professional truffle hunter, explain how he and his trained dog hunt for these buried morsels, which can weigh between two and four ounces and fetch up to 800 dollars a pound. Even better, visitors will learn how even a bare sprinkling of paper-thin slices from a white truffle of Piemonte weaves layers of rich flavors throughout the local cuisine.

TAGLIATELLE AL TARTUFO BIANCO
tagliatelle pasta with white truffles

SERVES 4

1/2 cup unsalted butter, divided
4 ounces white truffles, freshly sliced, or sliced and packaged in oil
1 pound tagliatelle pasta
1 cup freshly grated Parmesan cheese

In a saucepan over medium-high heat, add 1/4 cup butter and sauté half of the truffles for about 2 minutes; set aside.

In a pot of boiling salted water, cook the pasta according to package directions, or until al dente.

Drain pasta and transfer to the sauté pan. Add the remaining butter and Parmesan cheese. Toss well and top with remaining truffle slices. Serve immediately.

cato del Tartufo

Tartufo

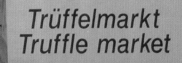

Trüffelmarkt
Truffle market

80 stand
enogastronomici

→

Degustazioni
Ristorazione
Musica
Folklore

In the world of gourmet foods, there is one Italian treasure

that is literally and figuratively worth its weight in gold—truffles.

Carpaccio di Bue al Tartufo Bianco

beef carpaccio with white truffles

SERVES 4

4 (3-ounce) beef tenderloin medallions
Salt and pepper, to taste
1/4 cup white truffle oil
1/2 pound fresh Belgium endive
16 slices fresh Parmesan cheese
2 lemons, halved

Line work surface with plastic wrap, approximately two feet long. Place one of the beef medallions in the center of the plastic. Place another sheet of plastic wrap on top of the medallion. Using a kitchen mallet, pound evenly until approximately 10 inches in diameter.

Uncover plastic wrap and place a dinner plate face down on top of the pounded fillet. Flip plate over with the bottom plastic wrap, allowing the pounded medallion to be in the center of the plate. Repeat above steps with remaining medallions.

On each plated carpaccio, sprinkle salt and pepper to taste, drizzle 1 tablespoon white truffle oil, and place a small handful of Belgium endive in the center of the carpaccio. Finish with 4 slices Parmesan cheese on top of the endive and serve with a side of lemon, and a drizzle of extra virgin olive oil.

RISOTTO AL PROFUMO DI TARTUFO BIANCO

white truffle risotto

SERVES 4

¼ cup extra virgin olive oil
½ medium white onion, diced
1 pound Arborio rice
Salt and pepper, to taste
½ cup white wine
6 cups chicken or vegetable stock
¼ cup unsalted butter
½ cup freshly grated Parmesan cheese
2 tablespoons chopped Italian parsley
2 ounces fresh white truffles, or sliced and packaged white truffles in olive oil

In a heavy bottom pan over medium-high heat, add the olive oil and onion and cook for 3 to 5 minutes. Add the rice, salt, pepper, and wine, stirring well. Continue to cook over medium-high heat for 2 to 3 minutes. Add the stock 1 cup at a time, as needed. Stir often so the rice does not stick to the bottom of the pan. Continue adding the stock and cook for 25 to 30 minutes, or until rice is finished cooking.

Remove from heat and add the butter, Parmesan cheese, and parsley; stir well to incorporate. Sprinkle the truffles over top and serve immediately.

CROSTINI AL TARTUFO

truffle crostini

SERVES 4

10 anchovy fillets
2 cloves garlic, crushed
1 tablespoon freshly chopped Italian parsley
4 tablespoons extra virgin olive oil
4 slices ciabatta, toasted
2 ounces white truffles, freshly sliced, or sliced and packaged in oil
½ cup melted butter

In a bowl, mix the anchovy, garlic, parsley, and olive oil (the anchovy fillets will be crushed while mixing).

Spoon the anchovy mixture on each piece of toasted bread and top with the truffles. Finish with a drizzle of melted butter. Serve immediately.

COMUNE
DI
CARIATI

The southern Italian region of Calabria has a rich heritage of architectural remains.

PARMESAN CHEESE FESTIVAL, EMILIA ROMAGNA

JUST AS IT IS RENOWNED for its treasured balsamic vinegar of Modeno, the Emilia Romagna region is heralded for what many consider the king of the world's cheeses—Parmigiano-Reggiano. Prized by chefs and home cooks the world over, this cheese is produced solely in the provinces of Parma, Reggio, Modena, and half of Bologna. This single product has an entire festival all its own—the Tradizionale Fiera del Parmigiano-Reggiano. Visitors will find the streets lined with stalls selling great wedges and entire wheels of the famous, aged mountain cheese, with the rich aroma of Parmigiano baking over a log fire in the traditional style, wafting over the entire town from its central square.

INSALATA DI FRAGOLE E PARMIGIANO-REGGIANO

Parmigiano-Reggiano strawberry salad

SERVES 4

8 to 12 fresh strawberries, stemmed
¼ cup pastry cream
¼ cup plain yogurt
4 mint sprigs, for garnish
8 to 12 slices fresh Parmigiano-Reggiano
Balsamic vinegar, as needed

Split each strawberry with a knife, but don't severe completely. In a small bowl, mix the pastry cream and yogurt until combined. Spoon the cream mixture inside each berry cavity. Garnish with fresh mint leaves.

Add one or two slices fresh Parmigiano-Reggiano into each cream-filled cavity. Plate the strawberries and drizzle with balsamic vinegar. Garnish the plate with more mint sprigs.

FONDUTA AL PARMIGIANO-REGGIANO

Parmigiano-Reggiano fondue

SERVES 4

2 cups heavy cream
1 cup finely grated Parmigiano-Reggiano cheese
4 tablespoons butter, cut into small pieces
Salt and white pepper to taste
2 egg yolks
Assortment of breads, breadsticks and blanched vegetables (i.e., asparagus tips)

In a saucepan over medium-high heat, bring the cream to a boil; add cheese. Whisk continually while adding the pieces of butter. Continue whisking, and add the salt and white pepper. When fully combined and melted, remove from the heat and add the egg yolks; whisk to incorporate.

Transfer cheese mixture to a prewarmed fondue pot and serve with various breads and blanched vegetables.

Italian cheese makers and Master graders take great pride in perfecting quality

cheeses, from **Parmigiano-Reggiano** to smoked mozzarella.

PROSCIUTTO FESTIVAL, FRIULI-VENEZIA GIULIA

FRIULI-VENEZIA GIULIA IS A diverse region stretching from snow-capped Alps, to rolling hills, to miles of scenic coastline peppered with resorts. While its cuisine is as varied as its geography, Friuli-Venezia Giulia is most renowned for a product coveted around the world:

its Prosciutto di San Daniele. Handcrafted by only a couple dozen producers, the ham is air-cured in the region's unique confluence of sweet mountain and sea salt breezes, producing a prosciutto like no other. The neighboring Carnia Mountains are home to a completely different but also much sought-after prosciutto: the Prosciutto di Sauris, which is smoked over a fire of beech wood and juniper berries. The wood and berries are in the fire, and produce the distinctive smoke flavor. Both of these treats are showcased at the appropriately named Aria di Festa—literally "Celebrations in the Air"—where these and other delicacies from the region are displayed, tasted, and admired from rows of colorful stalls, with sounds of musical entertainment and the cheering of sporting games in the background.

Prosciutto con Melone
fresh cantaloupe with sliced prosciutto

SERVES 4

1 cantaloupe, sliced into 8 thick
wedges (rind removed)
8 to 12 slices prosciutto
Extra virgin olive oil, as needed
1 teaspoon dried oregano

Plate 2 slices of melon on four individual serving dishes.

On each plate, wrap (or drape) 1 or 2 slices prosciutto around
or over each melon slice.

Drizzle with the olive oil and sprinkle with the dried oregano.
Serve chilled.

Asparagi al Prosciutto
asparagus wrapped in prosciutto

SERVES 4

12 fresh asparagus spears, cleaned
and bottoms removed
4 slices prosciutto
8 tablespoons butter
3/4 cup freshly grated Parmesan cheese
1 cup heavy cream
Salt and white pepper to taste

Preheat oven to 375 degrees F. In a steamer, steam asparagus for about
3 minutes. Remove asparagus and immediately submerge in an ice-water
bath to stop the cooking process. After several minutes, remove the
asparagus, pat dry, and set aside.

Wrap 3 asparagus spears with 1 prosciutto slice. Place on a nonstick baking sheet and bake in oven for about 4 minutes.

Meanwhile, in a saucepan, heat the butter, Parmesan cheese, cream, salt,
and pepper; stir until well combined.

Remove asparagus from oven and transfer to a serving platter. Drizzle
the sauce over each spear. Serve immediately.

 ALAMI FESTIVAL, CAMPANIA

"FOR THE INHABITANTS OF AMALFI who go to Heaven, it will just be a day like any other," Italian poet Renato Fucini wrote after visiting Amalfi, one of Campania's most magical cities. The same could be said for just about any town, vista, or even curve in the road of this stunningly beautiful region, which draws tourists from all over the globe. But in addition to the attractions of picturesque villages clinging to rocky cliffs, the sweeping blue sea, and the many places to soak up the warm Mediterranean sun on a sugar-sand beach, the culinary culture of Campania's coast is

increasingly being recognized as another jewel in the area's crown. One such food that has made its celebrated mark in this region—along with buffalo mozzarella—is the salami. As elsewhere in Italy where poverty and adversity have spurred development of some of its most famous foods, salami became popular amongst Italian peasants as a way to keep meat without refrigeration for long periods—often up to one year—supplementing a meager and inconstant supply of fresh meat. Today, traditional salamis—often named after the region or country of their origin, such as Genoa and Milano—are made not only from beef and pork but mixtures that may include goat, goose, lamb, poultry, and venison. The inconspicuous Salami Festival gives visitors a chance to sample these and many other varieties, as well as attend workshops on curing, smoking, and cooking.

Cured, air-dried salamis like Genoa

or Milano are often named after the region or country of their origin.

Bocconcini di Salame e Cipolla

Italian salami with green onions and mascarpone cheese

SERVES 4

12 slices Italian salami
1/2 cup mascarpone cheese
12 green onions, stems only
Extra virgin olive oil, as needed
Red wine vinegar, as needed

Top each salami slice with 1 teaspoon mascarpone cheese.

Place a green onion stem on top of each teaspoon of cheese. Fold each salami slice in a half-moon shape. Finish by drizzling the olive oil and red wine vinegar over top. Secure with toothpicks if desired.

Piadina con Salame

Italian salami flatbread sandwich

SERVES 4

1 cup pastry flour
1 cup all-purpose flour
1 cup durum flour
1/4 cup extra virgin olive oil
1 cup warm water
2 tablespoons salt
16 slices Italian salami
8 slices fontina cheese
1 cup fresh arugula

In a stand mixer with the hook attachment, combine the three flours, olive oil, warm water, and salt; mix until a dough ball is achieved. Remove the dough and knead on a floured surface for 3 to 4 minutes. Let the dough rest for 5 minutes and then divide into four pieces.

On a floured surface, use a rolling pin to roll out each dough ball to 7 or 8 inches in diameter.

In a large nonstick frying pan over high heat, cook each piece of dough for 3 minutes on each side.

Place 4 slices salami, 2 slices cheese, and 1/4 cup arugula inside each flatbread. Finish by folding the bread in a half-moon shape and pinch the ends to seal. Serve hot.

The Salami Festival is a culinary tourist event offering a wide selection of

high-quality salamis and sausages.

SNAIL FESTIVAL, LIGURIA

HAVE SNAILS COME to your local supermarket yet? They have in Italy. In Liguria, as well as Sardinia and Sicily, snails are a popular food, often found live in the supermarket near the partially refrigerated vegetable section—making them one of the few food organisms sold live at supermarkets. Snails can be cooked in an amazingly diverse number of ways, and visitors who come to the popular Snail Festival in Liguria are likely to have a chance to sample many, such as boiled with vinegar; in a casserole with squash, tomato, and potato; quickly fried in olive oil with lemon; or simmered in a rich tomato sauce with oil, garlic, and parsley.

LUMACHE AL GORGONZOLA DOLCE
snails with sweet Gorgonzola

SERVES 4

2 dozen fresh or canned snails, drained
1/2 pound sweet Gorgonzola
2 tablespoons freshly chopped Italian parsley
3 egg yolks
3 tablespoons unsalted butter
Pinch of nutmeg
1/4 cup chopped spinach
2 dozen snail shells

Preheat oven to broil.

In a bowl, combine the snails, Gorgonzola, parsley, egg yolks, butter, nutmeg, and spinach; mix well.

Stuff the shells with the snail mixture and place on a baking sheet. Broil in the oven for about 5 minutes, or until cheese is melted. Serve immediately.

LUMACHE CON BASILICO

snails tossed with pesto

SERVES 4

BASIL PESTO
2 cups packed fresh basil leaves
1/2 cup extra virgin olive oil
2 tablespoons pine nuts
1/2 cup freshly grated Parmesan cheese
2 cloves garlic, minced
Salt and pepper, to taste

SNAILS
2 dozen fresh or canned snails, drained
2 tablespoons unsalted butter
1 clove garlic, minced
Salt and pepper, to taste
2 dozen snail shells
1/2 cup freshly grated Parmesan cheese

Preheat oven to broil.

Combine all Basil Pesto ingredients in a blender or food processor; set aside.

In a sauté pan, sauté the snails with the butter and garlic for 2 or 3 minutes. Remove from heat and let cool.

In a bowl, toss the snails in salt and pepper and then stuff each shell with one snail and top with a spoonful of Basil Pesto. Place the snails in a casserole dish and sprinkle the Parmesan cheese. Broil on the middle oven rack for about 5 minutes, or until cheese is completely melted. Serve immediately.

TRADITIONAL CHESTNUT HUNT, VALLE D'AOSTA

VALLE D'AOSTA—the smallest and least populated region in Italy—is a land where nature is still uncontrolled: floral meadows, shimmering glacial lakes, and snow-capped peaks. The foods of Valle d'Aosta are as hearty as its landscape, a simple yet robust cooking influenced by the bordering French and Swiss cuisines as well as the cold, northern climate. The region is famous for its Fontina and Fromadzo cheeses, but is even more proud of its chestnuts. Valle d'Aosta's climate and locale are perfect for raising these rich, luscious nuts, and the region hosts the Traditional Chestnut Hunt to show the world the many creative ways the cooks of Valle d'Aosta prepare these delectable treats.

FRITTATA DI CASTAGNE
chestnut omelet

SERVES 4

1 (15-ounce) jar premium peeled chestnuts
6 eggs
3 tablespoons whole milk
4 tablespoons grated Parmesan cheese
Salt and pepper, to taste
1/4 cup olive oil

Purée the chestnuts in a blender until smooth.

Whisk the eggs and then add the milk, cheese, salt, pepper, and puréed chestnuts; set aside.

In a nonstick pan over medium-high heat, add the olive oil. Add the egg mixture to the pan and lower the heat to medium. Cook for about 8 minutes and turn over to cook the other side (another 5 to 8 minutes). Remove from heat and plate. Serve hot or at room temperature.

ZUPPA DI CASTAGNE CON PORCINI
chestnut and porcini mushroom soup

SERVES 4

5 tablespoons extra virgin olive oil, divided
1 small onion, chopped
1 potato, chopped
1 (15-ounce) jar premium peeled chestnuts
2 stems fresh rosemary
4 cups vegetable stock
1 clove garlic, diced
4 ounces fresh porcini mushrooms, sliced
Salt and pepper, to taste
Truffle oil, as needed

In a saucepan, warm 4 tablespoons olive oil over medium-high heat. Add the onion and potato. Allow to cook while stirring occasionally for about 5 minutes. Add the chestnuts, rosemary, and vegetable stock. Bring to a boil and reduce the heat to low. Cook for about 45 minutes.

Meanwhile, in a sauté pan over medium-high heat, add the remaining olive oil, garlic, and mushrooms. Allow to cook for about 2 minutes. Add the salt and pepper; set aside.

After the soup has cooked for 45 minutes, remove the rosemary sprigs and discard. Purée the soup in a blender, adding vegetable stock to thin if the soup is too thick.

Add the sautéed mushrooms and garlic to the soup; stir to incorporate. Transfer soup to individual bowls and garnish with truffle oil. Serve hot.

PART TWO: *Primi*

BEAN FEST 96
Linguine con Crema di Fagioli Vongole Gamberetti *seafood linguine with white cannellini beans*
Crema di Fagioli con Frutti di Mare *seafood and white bean soup*

GNOCCHETTI FESTIVAL 102
Gnocchetti ai Gamberi e Zucchini *gnocchetti with shrimp and zucchini*
Gnocchetti alla Vesuviana *neapolitan gnocchetti*

HERB FESTIVAL 106
Tagliatelle di Spinaci al Pesto *spinach tagliatelle with pesto*
Gnocchi al Pesto e Gorgonzola *gnocchi with Gorgonzola and pesto*

LENTIL FESTIVAL 110
Pappardelle con Lentiche e Pancetta Affumicata *pappardelle pasta with lentils and smoked pancetta*
Zuppa di Lenticchie *lentil soup*

MACARONI FESTIVAL 114
Maccheroni con le Triglie *macaroni with red mullet*
Pasticcio di Maccheroni *baked macaroni pie*

MUSHROOM FESTIVAL 118
Pappardelle ai Funghi Porcini *pappardelle pasta with porcini mushrooms*
Bavette con Prosciutto Cotto a Gallinacci *bavette pasta with brandy, roasted prosciutto, and chanterelle mushrooms*

OMELET FESTIVAL 122
Frittata di Gamberetti *shrimp omelet*
Frittata con Ricotta e Salsiccia *sausage and ricotta cheese omelet*

ONION FAIR 124
Pasta alla Cipolla Rossa e Ricotta *ziti pasta with red onion and ricotta cheese*
Pappardelle con Cipolla Rossa e Speck *pappardelle pasta with red onions and speck*

PASTA FESTIVAL 128
Spaghettata con Salsiccia *spaghetti with sweet Italian sausage*
Pici al Sugo Finto *pici pasta in a Tuscan sauce*

PIZZA FEST 138
Impasto per Pizze *fresh pizza dough*
Pizza Margherita *pizza with tomato, mozzarella, and basil*
Salsa di Pomodoro per Pizze *fresh pizza sauce*
Pizza con Prosciutto e Carciofi *pizza with prosciutto and artichoke*

POLENTA FESTIVAL 148
Polenta con Crema di Gorgonzola *polenta with Gorgonzola cream*
Polenta con Ragu di Agnello *polenta lamb ragu*

PUMPKIN FESTIVAL 150
Risotto con Zucca e Gamberetti di Fiume *risotto with pumpkin and crawfish*
Tortelloni di Zucca *handcrafted tortelloni filled with pumpkin*

Bean Fest, Basilicata

SOME OF THE MOST STUNNING SCENERY in southern Italy is tucked away in the heart of the tranquil, sun-drenched Basilicata region. The expanses of golden wheat near Potenza, the spectacular lakes around Venosa, and the picturesque towns that dot the hillsides have inspired many famous photographers and directors to use the area as a setting for their work, including Pier Paolo Pasolini, Francesco Rosi, Lina Wertmuller, and even Mel Gibson with his film *The Passion of the Christ*. Perhaps it is this extraordinary setting that has also inspired Basilicata's cooks to do so much with what some might consider a mild, even bland, primary ingredient—fagioli, or beans. For there is nothing bland about the ways this regional cuisine uses the versatility of beans, which can be found in a bewildering variety of colors, shapes, and sizes in the many local markets. Nowhere is this variety better showcased than at the popular Bean Fest—a grand, open-air event that celebrates the area's culture as well as its local food and wine. Here, visitors can wander among stalls featuring the beans themselves, along with others that serve them prepared in the local ways, often accompanied by cheeses, honey, and fruits. The Bean Fest is a must for anyone visiting Basilicata.

Linguine con Crema di Fagioli Vongole Gamberetti

seafood linguine with white cannellini beans

SERVES 4

2 (15-ounce) cans cannellini beans
1/4 cup extra virgin olive oil
3 cloves garlic
1 tablespoon freshly chopped Italian parsley, plus 1 teaspoon for garnish
1 pinch crushed red pepper
1 pound linguine pasta
1/4 cup white wine
Pinch of salt and pepper
20 manila clams
20 shrimp, peeled and deveined

Drain and rinse beans with cold water. Purée in a blender until smooth; set aside.

In a saucepan over medium-high heat, add the olive oil, garlic, parsley, and crushed red pepper; cook for 2 minutes. Meanwhile, in a pot of boiling salted water, cook the pasta according to package directions.

Add the puréed beans to oil and spices and cook for 5 minutes. Add wine, salt, pepper, and clams. Cook, covered, until all the clams open (discard any un-open shells). Add the shrimp and cook for 3 minutes. Drain pasta when finished cooking and transfer to a large serving dish. Toss with the beans and seafood, and garnish with parsley. Serve immediately.

Italy's Bean Fest is an opportunity to sample many of the country's beans.

POP CORN
€-1.30 k

PISELLI
€-1.30 kg

FAGIOLI
DARK
ROSSI
€-1.50 kg

SOIA
ROSSA
€-1.50 kg

corns, and lentils used in traditional soups, salads, and main dishes.

CREMA DI FAGIOLI CON FRUTTI DI MARE

seafood and white bean soup

SERVES 4

2 (15-ounce) cans cannellini beans,
¼ cup extra virgin olive oil,
plus more for garnish
3 cloves garlic
1 pinch crushed red pepper
Salt to taste
1 cup water or fish stock
1 tablespoon white wine
12 manila clams
12 mussels
12 shrimp, peeled and deveined
4 tablespoons freshly chopped Italian parsley

Drain and rinse beans with cold water; set aside. Purée in a blender until smooth; set aside.

In a saucepan over medium heat, add the olive oil and garlic and cook for 2 minutes.

Add the crushed red pepper, salt, and water or stock. Add more or less water or stock depending on whether a thick or thin soup is desired. Cook for 15 minutes.

Add the puréed beans, wine, and seafood, and cook, covered, until all the clams and mussels open (discard any un-open shells).

Transfer the soup to individual bowls and top with the parsley and a drizzle of olive oil. Serve immediately with toasted bread.

GNOCCHETTI FESTIVAL, CAMPANIA

CAMPANIA IS ANYTHING BUT a wealthy region, and here the first course of the typical Italian meal—often an economical pasta dish—has taken on a special importance. Driven by the need to make much out of little, the cooks of Campania responded by creating a diverse panoply of handcrafted pastas, each shaped to take advantage of specific sauces. While the region is also known for its savory seafood dishes, the importance of its pasta is illustrated by the fact that an entire festival is devoted to celebrating—not pasta generally—but a single, specific shape of pasta: gnocchetti. Gnocchetti is shaped like a curved shell, perfect for cupping the chunkier parts of a sauce, with ridges on the shell's outer surface to capture just the right amount of savory liquid. Gnocchetti is best paired with heavy sauces, as is deliciously demonstrated at the region's annual Gnocchetti Festival. Gnocchetti is a smaller version of the dried gnocchi pasta available in today's grocery stores. For home cooks who want to enjoy this distinctive pasta but have difficulty finding it, cavatelli and malloreddus are close substitutes.

GNOCCHETTI AI GAMBERI E ZUCCHINI
gnocchetti with shrimp and zucchini

SERVES 4

1/2 cup extra virgin olive oil, divided

2 cloves garlic

2 zucchini, washed, peeled, and julienned

Pinch of crushed red pepper

Salt and pepper, to taste

1/4 cup dry white wine

16 peeled shrimp

1 pound gnocchetti

Fresh basil leaves, chopped, for garnish

In a saucepan over medium-high heat, add 1/4 cup olive oil and garlic. Cook until garlic is soft and golden. Add the zucchini and cook for 1 minute. Add the crushed red pepper, salt, pepper, wine, and shrimp.

Meanwhile, cook the gnochetti in boiling salted water according to the package directions; drain and add to the shrimp sauce. Add the remaining olive oil and toss well. Top with basil and serve immediately.

GNOCCHETTI ALLA VESUVIANA
neapolitan gnocchetti

SERVES 4

¼ cup extra virgin olive oil
2 cloves garlic, minced
1 cup chopped Italian cherry tomatoes
1 pound gnocchetti
½ cup freshly diced mozzarella di bufala
¼ cup freshly grated Parmesan cheese
Salt and pepper, to taste

In a saucepan over medium-high heat, add the olive oil and garlic. Cook for 1 minute or until garlic is soft and golden. Add the tomatoes and cook for an additional 10 minutes.

Meanwhile, cook the pasta in boiling salted water according to the package directions; drain. Add pasta to the tomato sauce and toss well. Reduce the heat to low and add the mozzarella, stirring constantly until cheese is melted. Add the Parmesan cheese, salt, and pepper. Toss well and serve immediately.

HERB FESTIVAL, LIGURIA

IT IS DIFFICULT TO IMAGINE Italian cuisine without what may be its favorite herb—the deeply fragrant, intoxicatingly complex basil. The small-leafed Ligurian basil, grown in regional herb gardens caressed by moist sea breezes, is arguably the best in the world. At the annual Herb Festival, these little leaves are at their peak and are used to prepare the most famous of Ligurian sauces—pesto. While many cooks now prepare this mix of basil, garlic, salt, pine nuts, cheese, and extra virgin olive oil in a food processor, the name pesto is derived from *pestatura*, which means to be ground in a stone mortar with a wooden pestle. Aficionados say a mortar and pestle—and much elbow grease—is the only way to bring the entire flavor out of the basil leaves. But the Herb Festival is much more than just basil. Fragrant plants and herbs of all varieties are on display and for sale throughout the various parks and streets, while many styles of pesto are available for tasting.

TAGLIATELLE DI SPINACI AL PESTO
spinach tagliatelle with pesto

SERVES 4

1 cup heavy cream
12 fresh medium-size shrimp, cleaned
1 cup Basil Pesto (see page 90)
1 pound spinach tagliatelle
Freshly grated Parmesan cheese, to garnish

In a saucepan over medium-high heat, add the cream until it just begins to boil. Add the shrimp and Basil Pesto; stir well.

Meanwhile, cook the pasta according to the package directions. Drain the pasta and add to the pesto sauce. Toss well and serve with Parmesan cheese sprinkled over top.

GNOCCHI AL PESTO E GORGONZOLA
gnocchi with Gorgonzola and pesto

SERVES 4

1 pound potato gnocchi
1 cup cream
4 ounces mild Gorgonzola cheese
1 cup Basil Pesto (see page 90)
Freshly grated Parmesan cheese

Bring a large stockpot filled with salted water to a boil. Cook gnocchi according to the package directions.

In a saucepan, heat the cream and gorgonzola over low heat and stir until the cheese melts; set aside.

Drain pasta and toss with the cheese sauce and then stir in the Basil Pesto. Top with Parmesan cheese and serve immediately.

Homemade marinara sauce, available at the

Herb Festival, is derived from *marinara*, the Italian word for sailor,

*L*ENTIL FESTIVAL, ABRUZZO

ABRUZZO IS A REGION RICH with complexity. Its geography varies from towering mountains to a dazzling seacoast, brought together by gently rolling hills. Its culture is a blend of tradition and modernity. And, predictably, its cuisine reflects this complexity. One example is the region's use of the lentil, which is a key ingredient in many of Abruzzo's oldest and most traditional dishes, along with being featured in some of the most modern creations of the local culinary scene. During the Lentil Festival held in Abruzzo, the featured variety is a small, black lentil that is loaded with more iron than the average lentil and consequently cooks quicker. During the festival, the lentil is the headline ingredient in a variety of dishes, but the local favorite is still the lentil soup, served in bowls or poured over bread and baked in the oven. Unlike American lentil soups, the Italian variety incorporates fresh pasta, making the soup heartier and more delicious, particularly during the cold winter months.

PAPPARDELLE CON LENTICHE E PANCETTA AFFUMICATA
pappardelle pasta with lentils and smoked pancetta

SERVES 4

3¹/₂ cups water
1 cup dried lentils
¹/₄ cup extra virgin olive oil, plus more for garnish
¹/₄ cup diced yellow onion
¹/₂ cup diced smoked pancetta
Pinch of crushed red pepper
1 pound pappardelle pasta (wide-shape pasta)
Salt and pepper, to taste
Freshly grated Parmesan cheese, as needed

In a large pot, bring the water to a boil. Add the lentils and cook for 15 to 20 minutes or until tender. When finished, remove from heat; drain the water and set the lentils aside.

In a saucepan over medium-high heat, add the olive oil and onion and cook for 2 minutes. Add the pancetta and cook another 5 minutes, or until pancetta begins to crisp. Add the crushed red pepper and the cooked lentils.

NOTE: Add 2 or 3 tablespoons of water if lentil mixture is too thick.

Boil pasta in salted water according to the package directions and drain.

Add the lentil mixture to the pasta and toss well and season with salt and pepper. Garnish with the Parmesan cheese and a drizzle of extra virgin olive oil. Serve immediately.

ZUPPA DI LENTICCHIE
lentil soup

MAKES 1 CUP

1/4 cup extra virgin olive oil

1/4 cup diced onion

1/4 cup diced celery

1/4 cup diced carrot

1 clove garlic, smashed

1 pound lentils

6 to 8 cups water or chicken stock

1 cup diced potato

1/2 pound spaghetti, broken into small pieces and cooked

1 small bunch fresh Italian parsley, roughly chopped

In a stockpot, add the olive oil and heat on high. Add the onion, celery, carrot, and garlic. Stir until vegetables are lightly golden, about 2 minutes.

Add the lentils and 6 cups water or chicken stock. Bring to a boil and reduce heat to medium; cook for 45 minutes to 1 hour. Add remaining 2 cups water or stock as needed. Add potato and spaghetti, and continue to cook for an additional 10 minutes. Top with the parsley just before serving.

MACARONI FESTIVAL, MARCHE

THERE ARE TWO REGIONAL cuisines in Marche: one that developed inland, based on the fruits of the land; the other that evolved on the coast, based on the fruits of the sea. In the inland areas, traditional baked first courses include *vincisgrassi*, a timbale made from strips of egg pasta and layers of meat with mozzarella and Parmesan cheese. Another specialty is maccheroncini di Campofilone, thin noodles that pair well with a collection of meat sauces. These and many other regional specialties can be sampled at the Macaroni Festival, but as the name suggests, the star of the festival is the celebrated macaroni noodle. In the United States, the name *macaroni* may awaken memories of a thin box of macaroni and cheese with a packet of day-glow orange powder to be mixed with milk into something vaguely reminiscent of a cheese sauce. One would search in vain for such a macaroni dish at the Macaroni Festival. Instead, visitors will discover a variety of fresh macaroni noodles paired with such enticing ingredients as fresh fish, wine, and garlic, along with many other local Marche specialties from both land and sea.

MACCHERONI CON LE TRIGLIE
macaroni with red mullet

SERVES 4

¹/4 cup extra virgin olive oil
2 cloves garlic, sliced
1 pound Triglie fillets (red mullet),
cut into cubes
¹/4 cup dry white wine
2 cups diced Italian tomatoes
Salt and pepper, to taste
1 pound macaroni
2 tablespoons freshly chopped Italian parsley
1 cup fresh arugula

In a saucepan over medium-high heat, add the olive oil and garlic. Cook until garlic is soft and golden. Add the fish and let cook for 1 minute. Add the wine, tomatoes, salt, and pepper; allow to cook for 15 minutes.

Meanwhile, cook the pasta in boiling salted water according to the package directions; drain.

Add the macaroni and arugula to the fish sauce and mix well. Top with the parsley and serve immediately.

Pasticcio di Maccheroni
baked macaroni pie

PIE CRUST
1 cup unsalted butter
2¼ cups flour
1 teaspoon kosher salt
1 teaspoon sugar
3 to 6 tablespoons ice water

HOMEMADE TOMATO SAUCE
¼ cup extra virgin olive oil
1 small carrot, peeled and chopped
¼ small yellow onion, finely sliced
3 (28-ounce) cans tomatoes, with juice
5 fresh basil leaves
Salt and pepper, to taste

THE FILLING
8 ounces penne pasta
1 cup Homemade Tomato Sauce
¼ cup grated Parmesan cheese
½ cup grated mozzarella
3 or 4 fresh basil leaves, chopped
Salt and pepper, to taste

Pulse the butter, flour, salt, and sugar in a Cuisinart until the mixture resembles a course meal.

With the machine running, pour in 3 tablespoons ice water and pulse. Add additional ice water if necessary, until the mixture forms a ball. Turn off machine and remove the dough ball. Separate in half and store in refrigerator for 30 minutes.

NOTE: Dough can be stored in refrigerator for up to 2 days.

Remove the dough from the refrigerator, and let sit on a floured work surface for 10 minutes. With a rolling pin, roll each dough ball into a 10-inch circle; set aside.

In a heavy stockpot, add the oil, carrot, and onion and cook over medium-high heat for about 5 minutes. Add the tomatoes, basil, salt, and pepper. Bring ingredients to a boil, and then turn heat to low and cook for an additional 20 minutes, stirring frequently to avoid scorching. If sauce is watery, continue to simmer for an additional 5 to 10 minutes. After cooking, set contents aside and let cool. When cooled, purée in a blender. This sauce can be made ahead of time and stored in the refrigerator.

Cook the pasta in a pot of boiling salted water according to the package directions; drain.

In a large bowl, toss the cooked pasta with the Homemade Tomato Sauce, cheeses, basil, salt, and pepper.

In a greased 8-inch pie dish, layer the bottom with one of the rolled doughs, like making a pie; fill the dish with the pasta mixture and then top with the second dough, using a fork to seal the edges. Bake the pasta pie in a preheated 375-degree F oven for about 45 minutes, or until crust is golden brown. Remove from heat and let cool before slicing.

MUSHROOM FESTIVAL, FRIULI-VENEZIA GIULIA

IF THERE IS A UNIFYING characteristic of the many regional cuisines of Italy, it is perhaps the simplicity of preparation of many of its most famous dishes. In Friuli, this approach is the hallmark of its cuisine. Here, friends and family gather around a special fireplace called a *fogolar*, which is often set in the center of the kitchen, where cooks grill whatever was freshest and best in the market that day: pork, chicken, root vegetables, or the hearty and heavily scented mushrooms that are one of the region's staples. A favorite activity of the area is strolling through the dew-laden woods with baskets, carefully unearthing edible wild mushrooms for grilling at the fogolar, used in a variety of antipasto platters or seasoned sauces, or simply enjoyed on hot, crunchy crostini. These fabulous mushrooms have spawned not one but two regional festivals. In May there is the Mushrooms, Woodland Asparagus and Mountain Radicchio Festival; and in September comes the *Festa dei Funghi e dell'Ambiente,* loosely translated as the Mushroom and Environment Festival. Friuli produces some of Italy's finest mushrooms, and visitors can discover most if not all available for tasting at these regional festivals, which also provide information about gathering and preparing the famous fungi.

PAPPARDELLE AI FUNGHI PORCINI
pappardelle pasta with porcini mushrooms

SERVES 4

8 tablespoons butter
2 cloves garlic, chopped
1/2 pound freshly sliced porcini mushrooms
Salt and pepper, to taste
1/4 cup white wine
1 cup chicken stock
1 pound pappardelle pasta (large fettuccine)
2 tablespoons fresh chopped Italian parsley
1/2 cup freshly grated Parmesan cheese

In a saucepan over medium-high heat, melt the butter and add the garlic; cook for 2 minutes. Add the mushrooms, salt, and pepper. Add the wine and allow to evaporate; add the chicken stock.

Meanwhile, cook the pasta according to the package directions. Drain pasta and add to the sauce. Add the parsley and Parmesan cheese and toss well before serving.

Bavette con Prosciutto Cotto a Gallinacci

bavette pasta with brandy, roasted prosciutto, and chanterelle mushrooms

SERVES 4

2 tablespoons butter

1/2 cup julienned prosciutto

1 clove garlic, sliced

1 cup sliced fresh chanterelle mushrooms

1/4 cup brandy

Salt and pepper, to taste

2 cups cream

1 cup beef stock

1 pinch nutmeg

1 pound bavette pasta (thin, flattened strands)

1/4 cup freshly grated Parmesan cheese

In a saucepan over medium-high heat, add the butter, prosciutto, and garlic and cook for 2 minutes. Add the mushrooms, brandy, salt, and pepper. Reduce heat to medium and add the cream, beef stock, and nutmeg and then continue to cook for 15 to 20 minutes.

Meanwhile, cook the pasta according to the package directions. Drain pasta and then add to the sauce; stir well to incorporate. Garnish with Parmesan cheese and serve immediately.

Golden chanterelles from Italy's Mushroom

Festival are simply divine and can be added as an ingredient to many dishes.

OMELET FESTIVAL, MOLISE

ACCORDING TO LEGEND, when Napoleon Bonaparte and his army were traveling through southern France, they rested one night near the town of Bessieres. A local innkeeper prepared Napoleon an omelet that so impressed him, he decided to share the culinary delight with his entire army—ordering the townspeople to gather all the eggs in the village and to prepare a huge omelet for his army the next morning. Omelets are a Molise favorite too, and a much-anticipated part of the local Omelet Festival is Molise's own version of the giant omelet, prepared in front of a large crowd before being served up to all festival participants. In addition, locals and visitors alike come together during this festival to savor a creative smorgasbord of omelets, from those made with liver to those filled with fruit, every imaginable kind of meat, and the Molise region's famous cheeses and fresh garden vegetables. ✢

FRITTATA DI GAMBERETTI
shrimp omelet

SERVES 4

5 large eggs
1 tablespoon freshly chopped Italian parsley
Salt and pepper, to taste
¼ cup freshly grated Parmesan cheese
1 cup small shrimp, precooked and chopped
¼ cup extra virgin olive oil

In a bowl, beat the eggs and combine with the parsley, salt, pepper, Parmesan cheese, and shrimp.

In a nonstick pan over medium-high heat, add the olive oil. When hot, add the egg mixture and cook for 6 to 8 minutes, or until golden brown on the underside. Flip over and cook the other side for 6 to 8 minutes. Remove from heat, cut into slices, and serve immediately or at room temperature.

FRITTATA CON RICOTTA E SALSICCIA
sausage and ricotta cheese omelet

SERVES 4

5 large eggs
Salt and pepper, to taste
1 cooked and dried Italian sausage, sliced (or use chorizo)
½ cup fresh ricotta cheese
¼ cup extra virgin olive oil

In a bowl, beat the eggs and combine with the salt, pepper, sausage, and ricotta cheese.

In a nonstick pan over medium-high heat, add the olive oil. When hot, add the egg mixture, and cook for 6 to 8 minutes, or until golden brown on the underside. Flip over and cook the other side for 6 to 8 minutes. Serve immediately or at room temperature.

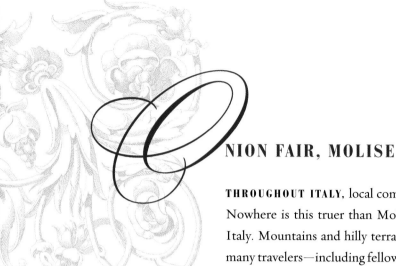

ONION FAIR, MOLISE

THROUGHOUT ITALY, local communities treasure culinary traditions rooted in local ingredients. Nowhere is this truer than Molise, the youngest, smallest and perhaps most isolated region of Italy. Mountains and hilly terrain have kept Molise separated from the rest of the country, and many travelers—including fellow Italians—have never visited here. As a result, Molise offers those willing to make the journey a remarkably preserved glimpse of days gone by—a land of ancient fragrances and flavors. The local Onion Fair is one example—a historical tradition that dates back to the thirteenth century, according to legal documents prominently displayed at the gastronomic celebration. Throughout Molise, the cultivation of onions is widespread and of all the many varieties, the red onion is the most common. The Onion Fair of Molise is one of the most dramatic and authentic illustrations of a local culture embedded in the local products of the land.

PASTA ALLA CIPOLLA ROSSA E RICOTTA

ziti pasta with red onion and ricotta cheese

SERVES 4

2 ounces pancetta, diced
1 pound ziti pasta
1/4 cup extra virgin olive oil
2 red onions, diced
1 cup ricotta cheese
1/4 cup grated Parmigiano-Reggiano cheese
2 tablespoons freshly chopped Italian parsley

Place the pancetta on a baking sheet and roast in the oven at 375 degrees F until brown, but not too crispy; set aside.

Meanwhile, cook the pasta according to the package directions; drain and set aside.

In a sauté pan over medium heat, add the olive oil and onion and cook until tender. Add the roasted pancetta and ricotta cheese and cook until cheese is melted.

Add the onion-cheese mixture to the pasta and toss well until incorporated. Top with the Parmigiano-Reggiano cheese and parsley. Serve immediately.

Pappardelle con Cipolla Rossa e Speck

pappardelle pasta with red onions and speck

SERVES 4

¼ cup extra virgin olive oil
1 large red onion, sliced
4 slices speck (juniper-flavored prosciutto), chopped
1 pound pappardelle pasta (large fettuccine)
Salt and pepper, to taste
4 eggs
½ cup freshly grated Parmesan cheese
1 tablespoon freshly chopped Italian parsley

In a saucepan over high heat, add the olive oil and onion. Allow the onion to sweat by cooking for 5 minutes. Add the speck and cook for 5 minutes more.

Meanwhile, cook the pasta in a pot of boiling salted water according to the package directions.

In a bowl, whisk together the salt, pepper, eggs, Parmesan cheese, and Italian parsley.

Combine the egg mixture with the speck and onions until incorporated. When the pasta is cooked, drain and add to the onion mixture; toss well. Serve immediately.

PASTA FESTIVAL, TOSCANA

TUSCANY IS A REGION rich in history, art, and tradition. Its capital, Florence, is the birthplace of both Dante and Michelangelo, and where Boccaccio wrote his "Decameron" and where Brunelleschi sparked the Italian Renaissance. Florence is also a fitting locale for a festival celebrating the quintessential Italian food—pasta. From classics like tortellini, cannelloni, and lasagna, to the specialized pici (handmade spaghetti from the Siena area) and testaroli (wheat pasta boiled and dressed with oil, garlic, basil, and pecorino cheese), pastas take all shapes and sizes, and most can be viewed, savored, and studied at the annual Pasta Festival. Even the simple boiling preparation of the pasta is an event at this celebration, where massive cauldrons are installed in the town square to prepare enormous portions of pasta dishes for everyone who attends.

SPAGHETTATA CON SALSICCIA

spaghetti with sweet Italian sausage

SERVES 4

15 to 20 fresh sage leaves, finely chopped
1 medium white onion, finely chopped
¼ cup extra virgin olive oil, plus more for garnish
4 Italian sweet sausages, casing removed and broken into pieces
1 pound spaghetti
Salt and pepper, to taste
Freshly grated Parmesan cheese, for garnish

Add the sage, onion, and olive oil to a saucepan over medium-high heat; cook for 2 to 3 minutes.

Lower heat to medium and add the sausage; cook until done, about 8 to 10 minutes.

Meanwhile, cook the spaghetti in boiling salted water according to package directions; drain. Add the pasta to the sausage sauce and toss well. Garnish with Parmesan cheese and drizzle a small amount of olive oil over top. Serve immediately.

Under Italian law, dry pasta, which is a work of art

in itself, can only be made from durum wheat semolina flour.

PICI AL SUGO FINTO

pici pasta in a Tuscan sauce

SERVES 4

3 fresh basil leaves
1 carrot, ground
1 stalk celery
1/3 medium white onion
3 cloves garlic
1/4 cup extra virgin olive oil
Salt and pepper, to taste
Pinch of crushed red pepper
1/4 cup white wine
2 (20-ounce) cans Italian puréed tomatoes
1 pound pici pasta (an unusual and
delicious cut of semolina pasta)
Freshly grated Parmesan cheese
Freshly chopped Italian parsley, as needed

In a blender or Cuisinart, blend the basil, carrot, celery, onion, and garlic until smooth.

In a heavy saucepan over medium-high heat, add the olive oil, salt, pepper, and vegetable mixture; cook for about 5 minutes. Add the crushed red pepper and wine and cook until alcohol has evaporated. Add the puréed tomatoes. Reduce heat to low and let simmer for about 45 minutes or until the sauce has slightly thickened.

Meanwhile, cook the pasta in boiling salted water according to the package directions; drain and add to the sauce. Toss well and then top with the Parmesan cheese and parsley just before serving.

Italy's wide assortment of pastas can be fashioned by hand

Pomodori
Cuore di bue

Cat. I   Italia
€ 6,80
                                          al chilo

SAN
http://web.ti
ORIGINE: VENETO (ITALIA) | CALIBRO
CATEGORIA   ‹II› | REG. OPER
                           | CENTRO

as the street vendors themselves.

PIZZA FEST, CAMPANIA

AS WELL-KNOWN AS CAMPANIA is for its pasta, seafood, and dairy products—such as buffalo mozzarella—there is another Neapolitan specialty loved the world over—Neapolitan pizza, the real symbol of the local cuisine. It was created in 1889, when Queen Margherita visited the area and a pizza maker from Napoli wanted to create a special pizza in her honor. Inspired by the tri-colored red, white, and green Italian flag, the pizza maker combined tomato, mozzarella, and basil on a thin crust and cooked it fast in a fiery, wood-burning brick oven. The result was a pizza that many aficionados still consider the epitome of pizza-dom. Every year, enormous quantities of the margherita pizza are baked at Campania's Pizza Fest, along with other pizza creations and Neapolitan dishes showcasing the region's bounty. The well-fed festival crowds dance to live music and cheer the pizza makers as they show off their dough-throwing skills, before indulging in yet one more slice.

IMPASTO PER PIZZE
fresh pizza dough

MAKES 6 (10-INCH) PIZZAS

1 package dry active yeast
2 cups lukewarm water
4 teaspoons sea salt
1 1/2 pounds all-purpose flour
2 tablespoons olive oil

In an electric mixer with the dough hook attached, stir yeast and lukewarm water until combined. Add salt and then add flour until dough begins to form and is not sticky, about 10 to 12 minutes.

Place dough in a bowl that has been lightly coated with olive oil. Also coat the entire dough ball. Cover bowl with plastic wrap and let rise in a warm place for about 1 hour.

Remove dough from bowl and place on a smooth working surface. Divide the dough into 6 balls, about 6 ounces each. Place each dough ball on a lightly floured surface and cover with a towel. Let rise for about 45 minutes.

One at a time, roll each dough ball on a floured surface until a thin 10-inch round pizza shape is formed. Store by simply freezing unused dough in plastic wrap.

RADIOKISSKIS

Sapori colori e tradizioni della Campania

Direzione Scientifica
Eugenio Luigi Iorio

Direzione Tecnica
Cosimo Mogavero

10ª edizione
GIFFONI
CITTADELLA DEL CINEMA

DAL 1 AL 9
SETTEMBRE

PIZZA MARGHERITA

pizza with tomato, mozzarella, and basil

MAKES 1 (10-INCH) PIZZA

1 (6- to 7-ounce) ball Fresh Pizza Dough
(see page 140)
1/2 cup Fresh Pizza Sauce (recipe below)
1/2 cup grated mozzarella cheese
6 to 8 fresh basil leaves
Extra virgin olive oil

Preheat oven to 450 degrees F with a pizza stone inside for 1 hour prior to baking.

While oven is preheating, dust a smooth working surface with flour. Place pizza dough ball in center and roll out evenly until about 12 inches in diameter.

Spoon pizza sauce evenly over top and sprinkle generously with the mozzarella cheese.

Using a pizza shovel, place the pizza on the stone and bake for 10 to 15 minutes, or until crust is golden brown.

Remove pizza from oven and sprinkle basil leaves on top. Drizzle with olive oil.

SALSA DI POMODORO PER PIZZE

fresh pizza sauce

MAKES 2 CUPS

2 cups tomato purée
2 tablespoons extra virgin olive oil
Pinch of dried oregano
1 clove garlic, smashed
Salt to taste

In a blender, add all of the ingredients and purée until combined. Store in refrigerator until ready to use.

There is no better place to enjoy pizza than at the Pizza Fest

in Naples—the city that gave the world this culinary phenomenon.

Pizza con Prosciutto e Carciofi

pizza with prosciutto and artichoke

MAKES 1 (10-INCH) PIZZA

1 (6- to 7-ounce) ball Fresh Pizza Dough (see page 140)
1/2 cup Fresh Pizza Sauce (see page 142)
1/4 cup grated mozzarella cheese
6 artichoke hearts, quartered and crumbled
4 large slices prosciutto
Extra virgin olive oil
Dried oregano

Preheat oven to 450 degrees F with a pizza stone inside for 1 hour prior to baking.

While oven is preheating, dust a smooth working surface with flour. Place pizza dough ball in center and roll out evenly until about 12 inches in diameter.

Spoon pizza sauce evenly over top and sprinkle generously with the mozzarella cheese. Arrange the artichoke hearts over top.

Using a pizza shovel, place the pizza on the stone and bake for 10 to 15 minutes, or until crust is golden brown.

Remove pizza from oven and arrange the prosciutto slices on top. Drizzle with olive oil and sprinkle with dried oregano.

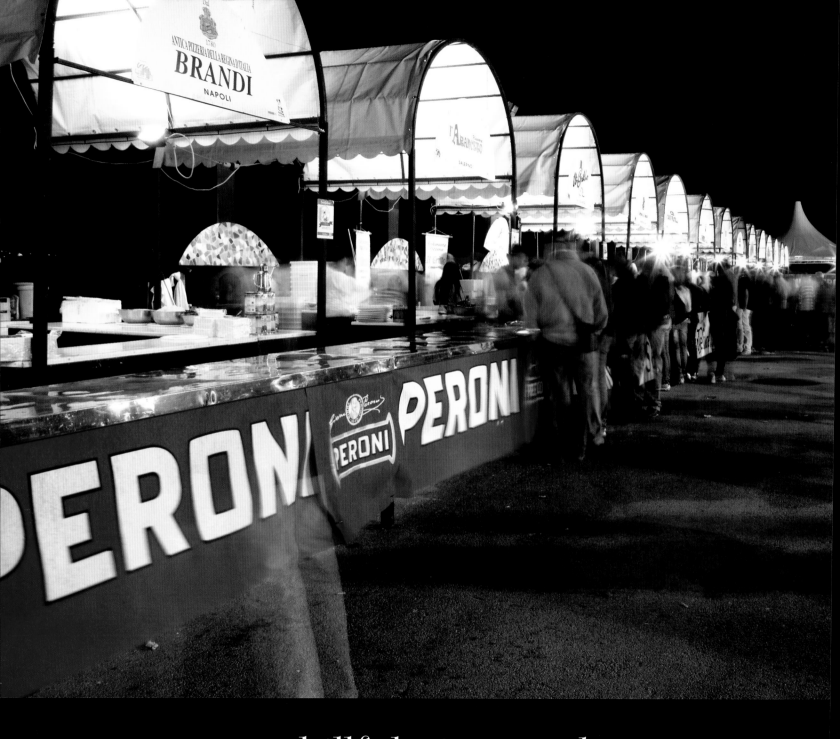

Learn skillful pizza-making techniques at the

Naples Pizza Fest, a celebration dedicated to the pizza in all its delicious forms.

POLENTA FESTIVAL, VENETO

VENETO IS A LAND of two distinct culinary traditions. One is the Venetian and Lagoon cuisine, which is based on exquisite seafood and a bevy of the finest vegetables. The other tradition arose in the inland regions where, shaped by long centuries of poverty, a peasant cuisine developed around the one ingredient most readily available—polenta. The need to devise unique ways to serve polenta inspired generation after generation of Venetian cooks to create a seemingly infinite variety of dishes for their families, all centered on this single ingredient. Much of this variety can be savored at Veneto's popular Polenta Festival, where polenta made with either white or yellow maize meal may be served as a creamy foundation for a fish or sausage dish, or grilled and served with pork chops, or richened with cheeses and laced with tomato sauces. Without question, polenta is a tasty canvas upon which Venetian cooks continue to create masterpiece after masterpiece.

POLENTA CON CREMA DI GORGONZOLA
polenta with Gorgonzola cream

SERVES 4

1 (16-ounce) box super-fine polenta
1 tablespoon extra virgin olive oil
1/2 tablespoon salt
1 cup heavy cream
1/2 pound Gorgonzola cheese, sliced and diced
Freshly grated Parmesan cheese, for garnish

Prepare the polenta by following package directions. Add the olive oil and salt to the cooked polenta.

In a saucepan over medium-high heat, bring the cream to a boil and then reduce heat to low. Add the Gorgonzola cheese and stir until melted.

Divide the polenta into four bowls and drizzle the Gorgonzola cream over top. Garnish with Parmesan cheese if desired. Serve immediately.

POLENTA CON RAGU DI AGNELLO
polenta lamb ragu

SERVES 4

RAGU
1/4 cup olive oil
1 cup each diced onion, celery and carrots
1 clove garlic, minced
1 pound ground lamb
1/2 cup white wine
1 (28-ounce) can tomato purée
Salt and pepper, to taste
1 bay leaf
Chicken stock (optional)
4 sage leaves, chopped fine
2 tablespoons truffle oil, for garnish

1 (16-ounce) box super-fine polenta
2 tablespoons butter
1/2 tablespoon salt
1/2 cup freshly grated Parmesan cheese

In a stockpot, add the olive oil, vegetables and garlic; cook over medium heat for 5 minutes.

Add the lamb and cook for 10 minutes, or until meat is crumbled. Add the wine and allow alcohol to evaporate. Add the tomato purée, salt, pepper and bay leaf. Bring to a boil, then reduce heat and simmer for 1 hour. If the meat sauce appears dry, add chicken stock, a little at a time.

Add the sage leaves about 10 minutes before cooking is complete.

About 5 minutes before cooking is complete, cook the polenta according to package directions. When polenta is finished cooking, add the butter and salt; stir well.

Divide the polenta on four plates and then ladle the Ragu over top. Garnish with Parmesan cheese, a drizzle of truffle oil, and serve immediately.

PUMPKIN FESTIVAL, FRIULI-VENEZIA GIULIA

IS A PUMPKIN A FRUIT, or a vegetable? Botanically, the pumpkin is classified as a fruit—it is the ripened ovary of a flowering plant. In the United States, the pumpkin is principally known for the glowing orange jack-o'-lanterns of Halloween and as the base for the delectable fall treat of pumpkin pie. In Italy, however, pumpkins are one of the most prized and versatile of fall squashes, nowhere more so than in Friuli. Here, pumpkins come in all shapes and sizes, from the common orange to dark green, pale green, orange-yellow, white, red, and gray. The dishes that Friulian cooks make from pumpkin are equally varied, from a rich stuffing for elegant ravioli dishes to a simple but delicious pumpkin soup. The annual *Festa della Zucca*, or Pumpkin Festival, in Friuli is a food and folklore celebration with colorful jugglers, knights, costume parades and wandering musicians playing medieval instruments. The pumpkin is the principal attraction, of course, featured as both food and ornament. Visitors can sample an array of local pumpkin dishes prepared exclusively for the festival and enjoy the elaborately carved and decorated pumpkins that appear throughout the towns and villages, all competing for a variety of prizes from most artistic design to simply the heaviest.

Risotto con Zucca e Gamberetti di Fiume
risotto with pumpkin and crawfish

SERVES 4

1/2 cup diced fresh pumpkin
1/4 cup butter, plus 2 tablespoons
1/4 cup chopped white onion
1 cup Arborio rice
1/4 cup white wine
3 cups vegetable stock
2 dozen fresh crawfish tails
1/4 cup freshly grated Parmesan cheese

Steam pumpkin for about 10 minutes by placing in a steamer over medium-high heat. When done, remove from heat and purée with a blender; set aside.

In a heavy-bottom pan over medium-high heat, add 1/4 cup butter and onions; cook for 4 minutes. Add the rice and stir. Add the wine and pumpkin purée and stir well. Add 1 cup vegetable stock at a time, allowing each cup to nearly evaporate before adding the next cup (this step should take about 15 to 20 minutes).

About 5 minutes before the rice is tender, add the crawfish tails and cook until the meat turns opaque. Add remaining butter and Parmesan cheese. Stir well and cook for 5 minutes more. Serve immediately.

TORTELLONI DI ZUCCA
handcrafted tortelloni filled with pumpkin

SERVES 4

FILLING
1 cup canned pumpkin
1 cup ricotta cheese
1/4 cup grated Parmesan cheese
1 tablespoon diced Italian mostarda
Dash of ground nutmeg
Salt and pepper to taste
Italian breadcrumbs (optional)

TORTELLONI
1 package large wonton skins
2 eggs
2 tablespoons butter
5 fresh sage leaves
3 cups cream
Salt and pepper to taste
4 amaretto cookies, crushed and crumbled

In a large bowl, mix all the filling ingredients together. If pumpkin mixture is very wet, add breadcrumbs until drier mixture is achieved; set aside.

To make the tortelloni, place wonton skins on a flat work surface. Using a 1-ounce ice cream scoop, place 1 scoop of pumpkin mixture into the center. In a separate bowl, beat the eggs for an egg wash. Using a pastry brush, dip brush into the egg wash and brush both sides of the skin or dough and fold into a triangle. Gently press around the filling area to remove any air pockets. Brush the two bottom corners of the triangle with the egg wash and pull corners together with one corner on top of the other. Repeat process until finished with the pumpkin mixture.

In a large saucepan, add the butter and sage leaves. After butter has melted, add the cream, salt, and pepper and then reduce the sauce by one-third. Meanwhile, in a large stockpot with boiling water, add the tortelloni and cook for about 2 1/2 minutes; drain and add to the sauce. Serve immediately with amaretto cookies on top.

The celebrated Pumpkin Festival is a delight for those fascinated

with Italy's colorful and versatile squash.

PART THREE: *Secondi*

ASPARAGUS FESTIVAL 156
Bocconcini d'Agnello e Punte di Asparagi *braised lamb with asparagus tips*
Involtino di Pollo con Asparagi *rolled chicken breast with asparagus, prosciutto, and fontina cheese*

BEAN FESTIVAL 160
Fagioli con Salsicce all 'Uccelletto *roasted Italian sausage with cannellini beans*
Aragosta alla Griglia con Fagioli all 'Uccelletto *grilled lobster with sage and cannellini beans*

BEEF FESTIVAL 162
Bistecca alla Fiorentina *porterhouse steaks florentine*
Bistecca alla Fiorentina al Chianti *porterhouse steaks with red wine*

DRIED COD FESTIVAL 168
Bacalla in Umido *dried cod stew*
Bacalla in Salsa Piccante *spicy dried cod*

FISH FESTIVAL 170
Totani con Melanzane alla Parmigiana *eggplant-parmesan stuffed calamari*
Branzino al Sale *salt-encrusted sea bass*

FROG FESTIVAL 180
Cotolette di Rana *fried frog legs*

RABBIT FESTIVAL 182
Coniglio al Vino Bianco *roasted rabbit in white wine*
Coniglio in Porchetta *roasted rabbit with herbs*

RADICCHIO FESTIVAL 184
Risotto all'Isolana *risotto with radicchio*
Gnocchi con Radicchio Scampi *potato dumplings with shrimp radicchio sauce*

SAUSAGE FESTIVAL 188
Peperonata con Salsiccia *Italian sausage and peppers*
Salsiccia e Rapini *Italian sausage with broccoli rabe*

SEAFOOD FESTIVAL 192
Canocchie con Aglio Olio e Limone *grilled shrimp with lemon and olive oil*
Scampi alla Griglia *grilled shrimp*

SWORDFISH FESTIVAL 202
Pesce Spada alla Ghiotta *braised swordfish with tomato and peppers*
Braciole di Pesce Spada *grilled swordfish rolls*
Pesce Spada alla Crema di Porro *swordfish with cream of leek*

TUNA FESTIVAL 206
Tonno al Cartoccio *tuna baked in parchment paper*
Tonno in Padella *tuna sautéed with white onions*

ASPARAGUS FESTIVAL, VENETO

WILD ASPARAGUS HAS long grown in the sandy soils throughout Italy and was highly valued by the Romans. In the 1700s, farmers of Argenteuil, northwest of Paris, began cultivating the lanky vegetable with great care. Word of their success quickly spread and soon the popular crop was grown—and prized—throughout Europe. In the Veneto region, tribute is paid to the asparagus at a festival all its own. Particularly popular at the festival is the tender white asparagus variety, which is grown almost exclusively around Bassano del Grappo on the River Brenta. To get its distinctive color (or rather lack of it), the farmer carefully covers the vegetable with dark plastic during the growing process, keeping the sun from reaching the stalk. At the annual Festival of the Asparagus, restaurants vie against each other with their latest green and white asparagus creations; the judges are the festival patrons who taste and vote for the most imaginative and delicious dishes. But for many local cooks, the traditional method for preparing asparagus is still the best: boil it to a perfect tenderness and then season it simply with a dash of salt and a drizzle of the finest, local extra virgin olive oil. One has only to close one's eyes to imagine the Romans enjoying it prepared exactly this way. Yet other cooks prefer the local Venetian seasoning, which is a sauce made of ground hard-boiled egg mixed with melted unsalted butter and a mixture of salt, pepper, and fresh minced thyme. *Bon appetito!*

BOCCONCINI D'AGNELLO E PUNTE DI ASPARAGI

braised lamb with asparagus tips

SERVES 4

¹/₄ cup extra virgin olive oil
1 cup flour
1¹/₂ pounds lamb, diced
1 cup dry white wine
1 sprig thyme
4 cups chicken stock
1 pound fresh asparagus tips
1 cup cream
Salt and pepper, to taste

In a heavy-bottom pan over medium-high heat, add the olive oil.

Pour the flour into a shallow dish and dust lamb pieces; shake off excess. Add to the oil and cook until golden brown, about 10 minutes.

Add the wine and allow to evaporate. Add the stock just until liquid covers the lamb. Reduce heat to medium, add the thyme, and cook for 50 minutes, adding more stock if liquid reduces.

During the last 10 minutes of cooking, add the asparagus and cream. Let cream reduce and remove pan from heat.

Season with salt and pepper. Serve immediately.

Involtino di Pollo con Asparagi

rolled chicken breast with asparagus, prosciutto, and fontina cheese

SERVES 4

8 (4-ounce) halved chicken breasts
Salt and pepper, to taste
8 slices prosciutto
8 slices Emmental cheese
8 sage leaves
8 asparagus spears
1 cup flour
1/4 cup olive oil
1 cup Marsala wine
1/4 cup chicken stock
6 tablespoons butter

Lightly pound the chicken breasts to tenderize; season with salt and pepper.

On top of each chicken breast, place 1 slice prosciutto, 1 slice cheese, 1 sage leaf and 1 asparagus spears. Roll each breast and secure with a toothpick. Dust the chicken roll in flour, shaking off the excess.

In a sauté pan over medium-high heat, add the olive oil and cook the rolled chicken breasts until golden brown on all sides; remove chicken from pan and let rest.

Deglaze the pan by adding the wine and allow the alcohol to evaporate. Add the chicken stock and butter, and cook until butter is melted. Add the chicken back to the pan and cook until chicken is moist and tender.

Transfer chicken to a serving dish, remove toothpicks, and top with the wine and butter sauce. Serve immediately.

At the Asparagus Festival, fresh, hand-cut spears are sold

in bulk, as are other produce specialties like Italian eggplant.

BEAN FESTIVAL, VENETO

FOR MANY TRAVELERS to the northeastern region of Veneto, their only stop is the timeless, beloved city of Venice, with its romantic canals, sleek gondolas, and enriching museums. But the adjoining areas of Veneto are equally enchanting. From magical Verona, immortalized in Shakespeare's *Romeo and Juliet*, to architect Andrea Palladio's stately Vicenza, Veneto's cities reflect the Venetian aristocracy that has populated this region for centuries. While the specific cuisine of Venice is known for its seafood and the surrounding areas for heavier, meat-laden dishes, Venetian cuisine is generally based on four basics: polenta, rice, vegetables, and beans. During the region's annual Bean Festival, visitors can select from a seemingly endless variety of bean dishes, including the classic pasta-and-bean soup, *pasta e fagioli*, which is a fixture in trattorias and a favorite on many family dinner tables across the region.

FAGIOLI CON SALSICCE ALL'UCCELLETTO

roasted Italian sausage with cannellini beans

SERVES 4

8 mild Italian sausages
3 tablespoons unsalted butter
12 fresh sage leaves
Pinch of crushed red pepper
4 cloves garlic
2 (15-ounce) cans cannellini beans, with liquid
Salt and pepper, to taste

Poke several holes into each sausage with a fork or knife. Roast sausages at 400 degrees F until the meat is cooked through, about 15 to 20 minutes.

While sausages are roasting, melt the butter in a saucepan over medium-high heat and add the sage leaves, crushed red pepper, garlic, beans, salt, and pepper; cook until creamy. Keep warm until ready to serve.

When sausages are finished, remove from oven and serve with the creamed cannellini beans.

Aragosta alla Griglia con Fagioli all 'Uccelletto

grilled lobster with sage and cannellini beans

SERVES 4

4 large lobster tails
1 bunch fresh tarragon
Salt and pepper, to taste
¼ cup plus 3 tablespoons extra virgin olive oil, divided
1 tablespoon fresh lemon juice
Dash of sea salt

CANNELLINI BEANS

3 tablespoons unsalted butter
12 fresh sage leaves
4 cloves garlic
2 (15-ounce) cans cannellini beans, with liquid
Salt, to taste
Pinch of crushed red pepper

Marinate the lobster with tarragon, salt, pepper, and 1/4 cup olive oil for 30 minutes.

Turn grill to high heat. When ready, grill the lobster tails until moist and tender, about 5 minutes (be careful not to overcook). Remove from heat and let tails rest for several minutes.

To prepare the beans, add butter and sage in a saucepan over medium-high heat. Stir for 1 minute and add the garlic, beans, salt, and crushed red pepper. Cook for about 10 minutes, or until beans are creamy.

To serve the lobster, place a bed of cooked cannellini beans on each plate. Top with a lobster tail. Whisk together remaining olive oil, lemon juice, and sea salt. Drizzle over top and serve immediately.

BEEF FESTIVAL, TOSCANA

NO DESTINATION EVOKES the romance, allure, and passion of the Italian experience quite like Tuscany. The ochre-tinted hills heavy with grapevines and fields of yellow sunflowers stretching to the horizon feel like an artist's imaginings, but are in fact the everyday backdrop for the Tuscan way of life. Tuscan cuisine absorbs the beauty of its surrounding landscape, manifested in Tuscan cooks' respectful awareness that the most important part of a meal's preparation takes place in the fields—the cook's job is to present these gifts of nature simply and at the peak of their flavor and wholesomeness. Visitors can experience a particularly savory exemplar of this culinary philosophy at Tuscany's Beef Festival, which, for the beef connoisseur, is the premiere must-go Italian festival. Here, Tuscany's famous specialty *bistecca alla fiorentina* is showcased—young beef steak from the Chianna breed of cattle, so named because they are raised in Tuscany's Chianna Valley. Local cooks set up a giant barbecue for festival participants and prepare thousands of steaks for the event: enormous T-bones and Porterhouse steaks so tender they require only a brief char over the red-hot charcoal fire, a sprinkling of salt, and a quick grind of fresh pepper. Squeezing a lemon and drizzling olive oil over the velvety meat is optional.

BISTECCA ALLA FIORENTINA
porterhouse steaks florentine

SERVES 4

2 (1½-pound) porterhouse steaks
Sea salt, to taste
Course black pepper, to taste
Olive oil, to taste
2 cups fresh arugula
1 lemon, juiced
Small handful of freshly shaved
Parmesan cheese

On a hot grill, cook the steaks on both sides to desired doneness.

Remove the steaks and allow to rest for 5 to 8 minutes.

Season the steaks with salt and pepper and drizzle with olive oil.

Serve the steaks on a bed of arugula. Top with fresh lemon juice, a drizzle of olive oil, and Parmesan cheese.

Many coveted recipes prepared at food festivals throughout Italy come from

family-owned bakeries, delis, and trattorias.

BISTECCA ALLA FIORENTINA AL CHIANTI

porterhouse steaks with red wine

SERVES 4

4 (1¹/₂-pound) porterhouse steaks
¹/₄ cup olive oil
4 cloves garlic, crushed
4 sprigs rosemary
2 cups Chianti wine
2 tablespoons Dijon mustard
2 teaspoons beef paste
Salt and pepper, to taste

On a hot grill, cook the steaks on both sides to desired doneness.

Remove the steaks and allow to rest for 5 to 8 minutes.

Meanwhile, make the sauce. In a saucepan over medium heat, add the olive oil and garlic and cook until garlic is soft and golden. Add the rosemary and cook for 1 minute. Add the wine and bring to a boil. Add the mustard, beef paste, salt, and pepper; stir well and reduce heat to a simmer. When thoroughly combined, pour over steaks and serve immediately.

DRIED COD FESTIVAL, LIGURIA

AN ENTIRE FESTIVAL devoted to . . . dried cod? American cooks unfamiliar with this internationally popular ingredient are in for a treat—and an education—if they can make it to the International Dried Cod Festival in Liguria, where dried cod's versatility and savory saltiness is celebrated every year. Attendees will also discover many other fish dishes of Liguria at the festival, such as ciouppin or cioppino, a soup with several kinds of seafood simmered with garlic, oil, and tomato. But the focus of the festival is definitely on the dried cod, which festival-goers can sample battered and fried in oil, served hot with a vegetable sauce, served chilled atop a crisp salad, or puréed into a wonderful cracker spread. When touring the region, keep an eye out for racks of fresh cod, split and salted, drying in the sun.

BACALLA IN UMIDO
dried cod stew

SERVES 4

2 small stalks celery, chopped
2 small carrots
1/2 cup olive oil, divided
1 medium white onion, sliced
2 cups chopped Italian tomatoes
Salt and pepper, to taste
2 pounds bacalla (dried cod)
1 1/2 cups flour
Freshly chopped Italian parsley, as garnish

In a Cuisinart, chop the celery and carrots. Transfer the vegetables to a sauté pan over medium-high heat and cook in 1/4 cup olive oil for 2 minutes.

Add the onion and cook for 3 minutes. Add the tomatoes, salt, and pepper. Cook until the onions are tender, about 15 to 20 minutes.

In a separate sauté pan, add the remaining olive oil.

Dust the bacalla in flour, shake off excess, and add to the oiled pan. Cook for 2 minutes on each side, or until golden brown.

When fish is ready, transfer to the sauce. Reduce the heat to low and allow fish to cook for 10 minutes. Remove from heat and transfer to a serving dish and garnish with the parsley. Serve immediately.

BACALLA IN SALSA PICCANTE
spicy dried cod

SERVES 4

2 pounds bacalla (dried cod)
1 cup flour
1/4 cup butter
1/4 cup olive oil
2 cloves garlic, minced
1 1/2 cups diced canned tomato
1 teaspoon paprika
2 tablespoons brandy
1 cup cream
Salt and pepper, to taste
10 green olives
2 tablespoons freshly chopped Italian parsley

Soak the bacalla in fresh water for 12 hours, changing the water every 3 to 4 hours.

Bring 8 cups of water to a boil and add the presoaked bacalla. Cook for 8 minutes. Remove the fish and let rest.

NOTE: Remove any bones and skin at this time.

Divide the bacalla into 4 pieces. Dust each piece in flour, shake off excess, and set aside.

Add butter to a sauté pan over medium-high heat. When butter is melted, add the bacalla and cook until both sides are golden brown.

In a saucepan over medium-high heat, add the olive oil and garlic and cook for 2 minutes. Reduce the heat to low and add the tomatoes; cook for 25 to 30 minutes.

To the saucepan, add the paprika, brandy, cream, salt, and pepper; stir well and then cook for 5 minutes. When sauce is finished, plate the bacalla and pour the tomato sauce over top. Garnish with the whole green olives and freshly chopped parsley. Serve immediately.

FISH FESTIVAL, SARDEGNA

THE BRINY RICHES that Sardinia's fishermen pull daily from the sea are too diverse, too bounti-ful and too delectable for just one festival. In addition to the Tuna Festival, the area hosts a string of other festivals and celebrations including the area's Fish Festival. Here, it is the sun-dried mullet roe and lobster that are highlighted, accompanied by savory fish soups like *fregula con cocciula* (broth with fregula and clams), *ziminu* (an old soup recipe containing various fish), and *agliata* (bean and mussel soup). If you attend, don't miss the *filetti di spigola allo zafferano* (sea bass fillets with saffron), as sea bass is a prized fish prepared in diverse and distinctive ways throughout the island. With Sardinia's numerous fish festivals, local seafood markets clustered around every port, and innumerable fish restaurants dotting the coastal roads, the island at times seems transformed into one big seafood restaurant—and one of the best in the world.

Pescheria " Paturzi"

DENOMINAZIONE COMMERCIALE

MERLUZZI

METODO DI
PRODUZIONE PESCATO

ZONA DI
CATTURA FA037(MEDITERRANEO)

PREZZO AL Kg € 8,20

Italy's countless Fish Festivals rely on local fishermen

to set the nets and deliver their catch every day.

Totani con Melanzane alla Parmigiana

eggplant-parmesan stuffed calamari

SERVES 4

EGGPLANT-PARMESAN

2 whole eggplants, peeled and sliced into
1/2-inch-thick slices
1 tablespoon salt
Pinch of sugar
4 cups olive oil, for frying, plus more
1 cup flour
5 cups Homemade Tomato Sauce divided
(see page 116)
1 cup freshly grated Parmesan cheese,
plus more for garnish
6 basil leaves

8 squid, cleaned, tubes and tentacles only

Preheat oven to 375 degrees F.

Place eggplant in a colander and sprinkle with salt and sugar. Set a plate on top of eggplant, allowing the extra moisture to drip out of colander.

Add the oil to a sauté pan over high heat and dust each slice of eggplant with flour. Add the slices to the pan and then fry eggplant until golden-brown.

In the bottom of a casserole dish, create several layers of fried eggplant and Fresh Tomato Sauce (using about 4 cups of sauce). Sprinkle with Parmesan cheese and fresh basil leaves. Repeat the same layer process. Bake for about 25 minutes, or until cheese on top is golden-brown; remove from heat and let cool.

When cool, spoon the eggplant mixture into a large piping bag or a ziplock bag with a corner snipped off with scissors.

Fill the squid tubes with the eggplant mixture. When filled, make a slit in the top of the stuffed squid tube with a sharp knife and add a tablespoon or two of additional eggplant-Parmesan mixture. Then re-attach the tentacle section to each tube by securing with toothpicks. Place the stuffed calamari in the casserole dish and drizzle with olive oil.

Return the dish to the oven and bake for about 20 minutes. When cooked, remove from heat and plate 2 calamari per serving. Top with the remaining tomato sauce and a sprinkle of Parmesan cheese before serving.

In northern Italy, fresh inshore fish and octopus are transported from the

boats to the kitchens, where they are added to hearty soups and spicy tomato-based sauces

Branzino al Sale

salt-encrusted sea bass

SERVES 4

2 whole branzino (2 pounds fresh sea bass),
cleaned with head attached
Extra virgin olive oil, as needed
Salt and pepper, to taste
2 cloves garlic, crushed
1 bunch Italian parsley, freshly chopped
4 pounds course sea salt
Lemon wedges

Preheat oven to 425 degrees F.

Lightly coat each side of the fish with olive oil and then season with salt, pepper, garlic, and parsley.

Coat each side of the fish with the salt, making sure each fish is entirely sealed. Transfer fish to a baking pan and bake for 30 minutes. Remove from oven and expose fish by cracking the salt crust with the back of a large spoon. Transfer the fish to individual serving plates and serve immediately with lemon wedges and a drizzle of extra virgin olive oil.

FROG FESTIVAL, LOMBARDIA

SIPPING A CAFÉ in Milan; sailing across the sun-strewn Lake Como; strolling the cobblestone streets of Bergamo's old city—the pleasures of Lombardia are many and varied. The best of old and new Italy meet here, from the fast-paced business and cutting-edge fashion center of Milan to stately lakeside villas and remarkable frescoes by fifteenth-century painter Mantegna in the Ducal Palace of Mantua. Although it is perhaps the most modern and cosmopolitan of Italy's regions, Lombardia still retains an age-old spirit that beguiles and delights. Nowhere is this more true than in the family kitchens of the region's nine provinces, where Lombardian cooks prepare traditional dishes with local ingredients like rice grown in the Po River Valley; fresh fish from the Po River, Lake Garda and Lake Como; choice salamis from Cremona; the world-famous *ossobuco* (braised veal shank); and fresh frog legs. Yes, frog legs. These amphibians are unmistakably—and deliciously— part of Lombardi's traditional cuisine. Attend the annual Frog Festival held in the outdoor garden of the town square, and discover new culinary delights as you sample such delicacies as fried frog legs, stewed frog and polenta, browned frog, and rice with frog livers.

COTOLETTE DI RANA
fried frog legs

SERVES 4

1 cup flour
Pinch of nutmeg
Salt and black pepper, to taste
12 frog legs
1 cup oil
1 lemon, for garnish

In a large ziplock bag, add the flour, nutmeg, salt, and pepper. Add the frog legs to the mixture and shake to coat.

When the frog legs are well coated, remove from the bag and fry them in a large fry pan filled with oil over medium-high heat. Fry until golden brown, about 5 to 7 minutes. When cooked, remove the legs and let drain on a paper towel.

Plate 3 frog legs per serving, and top with black pepper and a squeeze of fresh lemon juice.

RABBIT FESTIVAL, MARCHE

FROM ITS APENNINE MOUNTAIN towns to its seaside resorts and fishing ports, from the villages peppering its green valleys to the flatland towns, inhabitants of the Marche region celebrate life, family, music, and food with both gusto and delight. Perhaps this geographic diversity is what causes the cuisine of this eastern Italian region to cater to a more sophisticated palate than some of its neighboring regions. With a penchant for all things stuffed, natives of Marche savor the complexities of roasted pork and rabbit combined with wild herbs, garlic, and a host of other local ingredients. During the annual Rabbit Festival in August, visitors can sample some of the region's most popular and traditional preparations of this ingredient, so sadly neglected in the United States. For those unfamiliar, rabbit is leaner than beef, pork, or chicken meat, and is not gamey with a mild poultry flavor. Rabbit is generally sold in three categories similar to those used for chicken. Rabbits in the first category are called fryers, which are young rabbits between 1 1/2 and 3 1/2 pounds, up to 12 weeks in age, with tender and fine grained meat. Next is the roaster, rabbits that are upwards of 4 pounds, over 8 months in age, with firm, coarse-grained meat less tender than a fryer. Finally, there are the giblets, which, like chicken, include the liver and heart. Visitors to the Marche's Rabbit Festival can find all three categories of rabbit, often prepared with garlic, vinegar, sage, rosemary, and wine.

CONIGLIO AL VINO BIANCO
roasted rabbit in white wine

SERVES 4

1 whole rabbit, cleaned
Salt and pepper, to taste
1 cup flour
1/4 cup olive oil
10 fresh sage leaves
4 cloves garlic, crushed
1/4 cup white wine vinegar
1 cup white wine, plus more if necessary
4 potatoes, diced

Preheat oven to 350 degrees F.

Section the rabbit with a cleaver, season with salt and pepper, and then dust the portions in flour; shake off excess.

In a heavy-bottom pan over medium heat, cook the rabbit in the olive oil until golden brown on all sides, about 10 minutes.

Add the sage, garlic, and white wine vinegar. Allow the liquid to evaporate. Add the wine and potatoes, and allow alcohol to evaporate.

Transfer the pan to the oven and cook for 50 minutes or until rabbit is moist and tender. If liquid becomes dry, add more wine.

Remove rabbit from oven and serve with the roasted potatoes.

CONIGLIO IN PORCHETTA
roasted rabbit with herbs

SERVES 4

1 whole rabbit, cleaned
3 cloves garlic
2 sprigs fresh rosemary
1 teaspoon crushed red pepper
4 fresh sage leaves
1 fennel bulb
2 tablespoons fennel seeds
1/2 cup extra virgin olive oil, plus 3 tablespoons
4 potatoes, quartered
Salt and pepper, to taste

Preheat oven to 350 degrees F.

Place the rabbit in a pot of cold water and soak overnight in the refrigerator.

To make the stuffing: Grind the garlic, rosemary, crushed red pepper, sage leaves, fennel bulb, and fennel seeds in a Cuisinart. Drizzle in 3 tablespoons olive oil while blending.

Remove the rabbit from the refrigerator and stuff the body cavity with the herb mixture. When full, secure the rabbit with toothpicks or string to keep stuffing from falling out. Place the rabbit in a roasting pan with remaining olive oil and the potatoes. Sprinkle with salt and pepper.

Cook the rabbit for 2 hours. During the cooking process, baste the rabbit two to three times. When finished cooking, remove from oven and serve.

RADICCHIO FESTIVAL, VENETO

IN VENETO'S CHARMING town of Asigliano, the region's most recognized vegetable is celebrated in a festival that boasts an old-world feel with a sophisticated culinary experience. The regional ingredient is radicchio, a leaf chicory sometimes known as Italian chicory that often possesses white-veined red leaves. Eaten raw, radicchio's taste is bitter yet spicy, and is often used to add color and distinctive zest to a variety of salads. When grilled or roasted, the radicchio flavor mellows and richens, yet keeps a hint of its spicy kick. Varieties of this prized leaf vegetable are named after the Italian regions where they originate. *Radicchio di Chioggia,* the most ubiquitous variety in the United States, is maroon, round, and about the size of a grapefruit. *Radicchio di Treviso* resembles a large Belgian endive, while *radicchio di Castelfranco* is snow-white and looks more like a flower than a vegetable. At the Radicchio Festival of Asigliano, these and other varieties of radicchio are on display and featured in many mouthwatering recipes, from radicchio risotto and radicchio crepes to radicchio pasta. Come to the village of Asigliano, near Vicenza, and enjoy the celebrated radicchio.

RISOTTO ALL'ISOLANA
risotto with radicchio

SERVES 4

1 green onion, chopped
Butter, to taste
1 cup fresh radicchio
Salt, to taste
1 cup red wine
Extra virgin olive oil, to taste
2 cups uncooked rice
4 cups chicken broth
Bouillon cube, to taste
1/2 cup slivered Monte Veronese
cheese (or Parmesan cheese)

In a saucepan over medium-high heat, sauté the onion with a little butter until lightly brown. Add the radicchio and let cook until the leaves begin to shrink. Add the salt and wine.

In another saucepan over high-heat, add some butter and olive oil and sauté the rice. Add the chicken broth and let boil. Add a pinch of bouillon to taste; reduce heat and let the rice cook. When rice is tender, add the radicchio from the first pan and toss well.

Plate the rice and top with cheese slivers. Garnish with a fresh radicchio leaf, if desired.

Gnocchi con Radicchio Scampi

potato dumplings with shrimp radicchio sauce

SERVES 4

2 cups heavy cream

Salt and pepper, to taste

1 cup fish stock

1 large radicchio head, halved and crumbled with fingers

8 large shrimp, peeled and deveined

1 pound gnocchi

Freshly chopped Italian parsley, as needed

Freshly grated Parmesan cheese, as needed

In a stockpot over medium-high heat, bring the cream, salt, pepper, and fish stock to a boil. When boiling, lower heat to medium and add the radicchio; cook for about 5 minutes. Add the shrimp and cook until tender.

Prepare the gnocchi by boiling in salted water according to the package directions. When done, remove from heat, drain, and add to the radicchio and shrimp cream sauce. Toss well and top with Parmesan cheese and Italian parsley. Serve immediately.

SAUSAGE FESTIVAL, CAMPANIA

TO MOST AMERICAN COOKS, there are only two types of Italian sausage: sweet and hot. As tasty as these fennel- and/or anise-flavored pork sausages are, they represent only a fraction of the delectable varieties of sausages available throughout Italy. A great place to savor some of the best of this sausage diversity is at Campania's Sausage Festival, held every August. As seen in other recipes from Campania, the region's cuisine is often simple in preparation yet boasts extraordinary aroma and flavor, mirroring the open good humor and unrestrained *joie de vivre* of the local inhabitants. The region's sausage is a perfect illustration, and at the Sausage Festival visitors will discover many colorful varieties, including *Biroldo* (sausage made from pig and cattle), *Cotechino di Modena* (fresh sausage made from pork, fatback, and pork rind) and *Nduja* (a cream and extremely spicy sausage).

PEPERONATA CON SALSICCIA
Italian sausage and peppers

SERVES 4

¼ cup extra virgin olive oil
2 medium onions, diced
2 pounds yellow and red bell peppers, diced
4 fresh basil leaves
Salt and pepper, to taste
1 cup tomato purée
8 Italian sweet or hot sausages

In a heavy-bottom pan over medium-high heat, add the olive oil and onions and cook 5 to 10 minutes, or until onions are soft and golden. Raise the heat to high and add the bell peppers, basil, salt, and pepper; cook for 4 to 5 minutes. Lower the heat to medium and add the tomato purée. Cook for 30 minutes, stirring occasionally.

Meanwhile, roast the sausages in the oven at 375 degrees F for 15 minutes, or grill them until done. Add the cooked sausage to the sauce and toss well. Serve immediately.

Salsiccia e Rapini

Italian sausage with broccoli rabe

SERVES 4

12 Italian sweet or hot sausages
1/4 cup extra virgin olive oil
4 cloves garlic, diced
6 bunches rapini (broccoli rabe), steamed
1/4 cup white wine
1 teaspoon crushed red pepper
Salt and pepper, to taste

Prepare the sausages by poking each link with a fork two or three times.

In a heavy-bottom pan over medium-high heat, add the olive oil, garlic, and sausage; cook the sausages evenly, about 5 minutes to brown the outer casing.

Meanwhile, prepare the rapini by steaming in a steamer or a wok with a small amount of water; drain and set aside.

Add the wine to the sausages. Allow alcohol to evaporate. Add the crushed red pepper and the steamed rapini; add salt and pepper. Cover and cook for about 2 to 3 minutes. Remove lid and continue to cook for 15 to 20 minutes or until sausage is cooked through. Serve immediately.

Campania's Sausage Festival features a bounty of

handcrafted sausage links and cured salamis.

SEAFOOD FESTIVAL, ABRUZZO

THE MANY EYE-CATCHING vistas of the deep blue Adriatic Sea off Abruzzo's coast are a well-known tourist attraction, but this nutrient-rich body of water is also home to a startling variety of marine life, which has become a major attraction in its own right. Every September, a visually striking Seafood Festival known as the Conocchie Procession pays homage to this bounty in a unique and attractive way: by fabricating fishing vessels from wheat and adorning them with colorful flowers and ribbons. Of course, fish of all kinds are on display and offered for tasting throughout the festival; visitors strolling through the stalls, shops, and restaurants will discover local dishes showcasing cod, cuttlefish, mullet, scampi, scorpion fish, and sole—to name only a few. And don't miss the seafood soups, with their exotic blends of fish and tantalizing Abruzzo ingredients such as the region's own extra virgin olive oil and spicy paprika.

CANOCCHIE CON AGLIO OLIO E LIMONE
grilled shrimp with lemon and olive oil

SERVES 4

2 pounds fresh shrimp, tails only, peeled
1 cup dry white wine
1 bunch thyme
2 cloves garlic
1 bay leaf
1 teaspoon black peppercorns
¼ cup extra virgin olive oil
1 bunch fresh Italian parsley, chopped
1 lemon, juiced

In a bowl, marinate the shrimp in the wine, thyme, garlic, bay leaf, and peppercorns for at least 1 hour.

In a small bowl, add the olive oil, parsley, and lemon juice; toss well.

Transfer the shrimp and marinade to a sauté pan over medium-high heat and cook until shrimp are opaque and tender. When done, remove shrimp from the pan and transfer to a serving dish. Top with the lemon and parsley sauce and serve immediately.

Pescheria " Paturzi "

DENOMINAZIONE COMMERCIALE

GAMBERETTI

METODO DI
PRODUZIONE _____ PESCATO

ZONA DI
CATTURA _____ FAO37 (MEDITERRANEO)

PREZZO AL Kg € _____ 8,20

At an Italian Seafood Festival, expect to find a bevy

with outstanding seafood year-round.

SCAMPI ALLA GRIGLIA

grilled shrimp

SERVES 4

2 pounds fresh large shrimp or prawns, butterflied, shells attached

1/2 cup extra virgin olive oil, divided

2 teaspoons freshly chopped Italian parsley, divided

2 cloves garlic, minced

1/3 cup Italian breadcrumbs

Salt and pepper, to taste

1 lemon, sliced into thin wheels

In a bowl, add the shrimp, 1/4 cup olive oil, 1 teaspoon parsley, garlic, breadcrumbs, salt, and pepper; toss well.

On an open grill, cook the shrimp and lemon wheels until golden brown.

Transfer the grilled shrimp and lemon to a serving dish and top with the remaining olive oil and parsley. Serve immediately.

Italy's architecture seems to have sprung uniformly from somewhere between the 12th

and 16th centuries and its secretive walls sparkle with flashes of water glimpsed through cracks and windows

SWORDFISH FESTIVAL, CALABRIA

ALONG CALABRIA'S SUN-SOAKED coastline, fish of all kinds is the quintessential food, and all of it is excellent. But there is one species of fish whose festival brings locals and visitors flocking every summer to the waterfront stalls to taste and pay tribute. Known as the gladiator fish because of its sharp bill, streamlined physique, and ability to slice through the water with powerful agility and grace, the swordfish is one of the most prized species in Calabria and is the superstar of its annual Swordfish Festival. Contrary to belief, the "sword" is not used to spear but rather to slash prey, often disabling it and making for an easier meal. Due to the large size of the swordfish, the prized meat is usually sold as steaks instead of fillets, perfect for grilling over a hot and smoky wood fire. The color of a swordfish's meat also varies by its diet; for instance, a swordfish caught off the east coast of North America is often much rosier than its Italian counterpart. But whatever the color, and whether grilled, sautéed, baked, poached, or braised by the inventive cooks of Calabria, the centerpiece of the Swordfish Festival is sure to delight.

PESCE SPADA ALLA GHIOTTA
braised swordfish with tomato and peppers

SERVES 4

¹/₄ cup olive oil
1 clove garlic, minced
¹/₂ white onion, julienned
¹/₂ red bell pepper, julienned
¹/₂ green bell pepper, julienned
¹/₂ cup tomato purée
Pinch of crushed red pepper
2 fresh basil leaves
Pinch of dried oregano
Salt and pepper, to taste
1 cup water
4 (6-ounces) fresh swordfish steaks

In a sauté pan over medium-high heat, add the olive oil and garlic; cook for 1 minute. Add the onion and bell peppers; stir well. Add the tomato purée, crushed red pepper, basil, oregano, salt, and pepper, and cook for 5 minutes. Reduce heat to low, add water and cook for 20 minutes more.

Add the swordfish steaks to the sauce and cook for 8 to 10 minutes or until fish is moist and cooked through. Remove from heat and serve immediately.

BRACIOLE DI PESCE SPADA
grilled swordfish rolls

SERVES 4

4 (6-ounce) fresh swordfish steaks
4 slices soft white bread
2 tablespoons freshly chopped Italian parsley
1 teaspoon capers
2 tablespoons extra virgin olive oil,
plus more for drizzling
Salt and pepper, to taste
1/2 cup chopped cherry tomatoes
1 tablespoon freshly chopped basil
1 teaspoon olive oil

Cut the swordfish steaks into thin slices and lay them out on a cutting board.

Begin the filling by crumbling the white bread into small pieces. Place the bread, parsley, capers, olive oil, salt, and pepper in a large dish; mix well.

Spread the bread mixture over each slice of swordfish. Roll each slice tightly and secure with a toothpick. Drizzle the top of each slice with a little olive oil.

Using a barbecue skewer, add the swordfish rolls to the skewers, removing the toothpicks when complete. Grill over an open flame until fish is moist and cooked through.

Meanwhile, toss the tomatoes in a small bowl with the basil and olive oil until well combined. Serve a dollop of the mixture alongside the swordfish rolls.

PESCE SPADA ALLA CREMA DI PORRO
swordfish with cream of leek

SERVES 4

10 cups water
Pinch of salt
1/2 white onion, sectioned
1 stalk celery, chopped
1 carrot, chopped
4 (6-ounce) fresh swordfish steaks
5 tablespoons butter
4 medium leeks, sliced
2 tablespoons flour
2 cups fish stock or clam juice
Salt and white pepper, to taste
1 red apple, skin removed, grated

Bring the water to a boil and add the salt, onion, celery, and carrot. Add the swordfish steaks and poach in the boiling water for 10 minutes.

Meanwhile, in a saucepan over medium-high heat, melt the butter. Add the leeks and cook for 7 to 8 minutes. Add the flour and stir well. Continue to cook for 3 minutes. Add the fish stock or clam juice and then add the salt and pepper.

When fish is finished poaching, transfer the steaks to a serving dish and pour the creamy leek sauce over top. Garnish with freshly grated apple. Serve immediately.

PESCE SPADA
PESCATO
MEDITERRANEO

Pesce Spada is Italian for swordfish—a popular fish

PESCE SPADA

Xiphias Glaolius   (Linneo 1758)

Pescato in Mare Mediterraneo

Alto Adriatico

in Italy that has an annual festival named in its honor.

TUNA FESTIVAL, SARDEGNA

GREATLY INFLUENCED BY its island insularity, Sardinia is a magical and charming land whose warm-hearted people have a long history of opening their arms to any visitor intrepid enough to reach its shores. Today, modern transportation has taken the "intrepid" out of the journey, but the hospitality of the people remains. Combine their gracious welcome with the island's landscape of incredibly diverse beauty, world-class cuisine, and age-old traditions largely unchanged by outside influences, and Sardinia is a world no visitor should miss the chance to explore. Surrounded as it is by the sea, local dishes naturally feature the daily catches that fishermen have been harvesting for generations. None is more popular with residents and visitors than the freshly caught tuna. A great way to sample the variety of methods Sardinia cooks have developed for preparing this popular finfish is at the Tuna Festival. Held every year in May, the festival stresses traditional as well as new tuna dishes, many exquisitely paired with Italian wines, all available for tasting. Other local fish dishes are featured, but it is still the tuna that will linger longest in visitors' memories, enticing them to return year after year.

TONNO AL CARTOCCIO
tuna baked in parchment paper

SERVES 4

4 (6-ounce) tuna steaks
1/2 cup extra virgin olive oil
Salt and pepper
4 slices lemon
4 anchovy fillets
2 tablespoons capers
16 black olives
1/2 cup halved cherry tomatoes

Preheat oven to 375 degrees F.

Fold some parchment paper to make four envelopes, about 12 x 16 inches.

Drizzle each tuna steak with olive oil and sprinkle with salt and pepper.

In each envelope, place 1 tuna steak, 1 slice of lemon, and 1 anchovy fillet. Divide the capers, olives, and cherry tomatoes evenly inside each package.

Seal envelopes and place on a baking sheet. Bake for 20 to 25 minutes; remove and serve immediately.

TONNO IN PADELLA

tuna sautéed with white onions

SERVES 4–6

¹/₄ cup extra virgin olive oil
2 medium white onions, thinly sliced
Salt and pepper, to taste
4 (6-ounce) tuna steaks
1 cup dry white wine
1 tablespoon dried oregano

In a large sauté pan over medium-high heat, add the olive oil and onions and cook until soft and golden.

Salt and pepper the tuna steaks and then set on top of onions. Add the wine and dried oregano and continue cooking until the wine is reduced, about 5 to 8 minutes. Remove from heat and serve immediately.

PART FOUR: *Dolce*

APPLE FESTIVAL 212
Torta di Mele Rustica *rustic apple torte*

CHERRY FESTIVAL 214
Ciliege al Vino Rosso *cherries marinated in red wine*
Crostata di Visciole *cherry crostata*

CHOCOLATE FESTIVAL 218
Mousse di Gianduia *chocolate and toasted hazelnut mousse*
Liquore al Cioccolato *chocolate liqueur*

DESSERT FESTIVAL 224
Biscotti alle Mandore *anise almond biscotti*
Gratin di Frutti di Bosco al Zabaglione *zabaglione gratin*

LEMON FESTIVAL 228
Frittelle di Ricotta al Limone *lemon ricotta fritter*
Sorbetto al Limone *lemon sorbet in lemon shells*

PISTACHIO FESTIVAL 232
Gelato di Pistacchio *pistachio gelato*

PRICKLY PEAR FESTIVAL 234
Soufflé di Fichi d'India *prickly pear soufflé*
Zuccotto di Fichi d'India *prickly pear cake*

STRAWBERRY FESTIVAL 238
Fragole con Aceto Balsamico *strawberries with balsamic vinegar and sugar*
Crespelle di Fragole *strawberry crepes with strawberry and port wine sauce*

STRUDEL, MUSCAT WINE, AND VIN SANTO WINE FESTIVAL 242
Strudel di Mele *apple strudel*

WATERMELON FESTIVAL 244
Macedonia d'Arancia Rossa *melon balls in blood orange sauce*
Granita di Cocomero *watermelon granita*

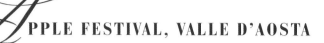

APPLE FESTIVAL, VALLE D'AOSTA

THE PRINCIPAL AGRICULTURE product of the picturesque Valle d'Aosta region is the apple—and so, of course, it must have its own festival. Held in October, the peak of the season, the Valle d'Aosta's Apple Festival celebrates the full variety of apples grown in the region, notably Renette, Jonagold, Delicious, and Starking. Whether baked in rich desserts like apple tarts and pies, bottled with syrup or wine, dried, or savored in all their raw crunchiness, the apples of Valle d'Aosta delight young and old, visitors and locals, and chefs as well as home cooks.

TORTA DI MELE RUSTICA
rustic apple torte

SERVES 8-10

2 fresh apples
1 small lemon
1 cup sugar, divided
3/4 cup unsalted butter, room temperature
4 large eggs
2 1/2 cups cake flour
2 teaspoons baking powder
1/2 teaspoon salt
1 1/2 teaspoons vanilla
1/2 cup whole milk
1/2 cup heavy cream
1 1/2 teaspoons cinnamon
1/4 cup powdered sugar

Preheat the oven to 350 degrees F. Butter and flour a 10-inch springform pan and line the bottom with parchment paper.

Peel the apples, core, halve, and thinly slice. Zest lemon, reserving zest. Squeeze some lemon juice over apples and toss; set aside.

In a large mixing bowl, cream together 3/4 cup sugar and butter at least 5 minutes, scraping the bowl as needed. Add eggs, one at a time, beating well between each addition.

In a separate bowl, sift together the flour, baking powder, and salt. Add vanilla and lemon zest to milk. Fold half the flour into the egg mixture and stir in half the milk. Fold in remaining flour and then stir in remaining milk. Pour the batter into the prepared pan and smooth the top.

Place apple slices in concentric circles on top of batter to completely cover the top of the cake and then pour cream over top. Mix together the remaining 1/4 cup sugar and the cinnamon and sprinkle over cream.

Bake until toothpick inserted into the center of the cake comes out clean, about 45 minutes. Transfer cake to a wire rack and let cool completely. Release from pan and slide onto a serving platter.

Cut into 8 to 10 wedges. Dust with powdered sugar; serve warm with vanilla gelato or as a coffeecake.

CHERRY FESTIVAL, VENETO

VENETO IS FAMOUS for its sophisticated desserts—heavenly creations like sweet lasagna prepared with poppy seeds and walnuts, and its renowned Christmas cake. But not all of the region's sweets are concocted by expert pastry chefs. Veneto's fresh fruits—crafted by nature, kissed by the sun, and brought to market at perfect ripeness—can hold their own against the most delectable products of a chef's oven. One such fruit is the Italian cherry, feted every year at the Veneto Cherry Festival. Here, visitors wander—intoxicated by the fresh, floral aromas and entertained by musical shows and the regional pageantry—weaving their way among over one hundred exhibitors' stands featuring a vast array of cherry dishes. And imagine: this indulgence is healthy! The red pigment in cherries contains anthocyanins, which have been shown to reduce pain and inflammation. These red jewels are also packed with potent antioxidants, and are used to treat gout—a painful inflammatory joint condition. A dessert one can enjoy without guilt!

CILIEGE AL VINO ROSSO

cherries marinated in red wine

SERVES 4

2 pounds fresh red cherries
2 cups fruity red wine
2 cups sugar
1 cup whipped cream

Wash and dry the cherries. Carefully remove the pits and stems; set aside.

In a medium saucepan over medium-high heat, bring the red wine and sugar to a boil. When boiling, add the cherries and cook for 15 minutes. Remove from heat and allow the cherries and wine to cool.

Divide the cherries and wine into individual serving bowls and top with the whipped cream.

CROSTATA DI VISCIOLE

cherry crostata

PASTA FROLLA

2¹/₄ cups all-purpose flour

¹/₂ cup sugar

¹/₂ teaspoon salt

¹/₂ teaspoon baking powder

³/₄ cup butter, cold and cubed

2 eggs, slightly beaten

1 teaspoon vanilla

1 teaspoon lemon zest

CHERRY FILLING

5 cups pitted fresh cherries

¹/₂ cup sugar

2 tablespoons cornstarch

1 teaspoon lemon zest

1 teaspoon vanilla extract

EGG WASH

1 egg

1 tablespoon water

Spray an 11-inch fluted round tart pan with a removable bottom with nonstick spray and then line with parchment paper.

Preheat oven to 350 degrees F.

In a food processor, add flour, sugar, salt, and baking powder; whisk to blend. Add butter and pulse about ten times. Turn mixer on and add eggs, vanilla, and zest and then pulse until it looks grainy. Turn out on a clean surface and knead into a ball; cut in half and shape into two 5-inch disks. Cover with plastic wrap and refrigerate at least 30 minutes. Remove dough 5 to 10 minutes before rolling time.

Roll out 1 piece of dough on a lightly floured surface, into a 12-inch circle. Trim edges, slightly, before lifting and placing over pan. Let edges hang over loosely. Roll out second dough into an oblong shape at least 12 x 14 inches. With a fluted pastry wheel, make 1-inch-long strips lengthwise to make twelve 1-inch strips.

In a bowl, mix together the Cherry Filling ingredients and then pour into tart pan with the dough. Brush the dough strips and edge of tart with egg wash, then in a lattice design, lay 6 strips down in one direction, 1-inch apart from each other. Then on an angle, lay the remaining 6 strips on top of previous strips. Press down to seal edges and remove any dough hanging off sides of pan.

Place tart on a cookie sheet and bake for 45 minutes to 1 hour, or until golden and bubbly; let cool. Garnish with powdered sugar before serving.

CHOCOLATE FESTIVAL, UMBRIA

"VERDANT UMBRIA" . . . "Holy Umbria" . . . "Umbria of a Hundred Towns" . . .Many aphorisms attempt to capture the essence of Umbria, but no single phrase can encompass this complex and diverse region. Like the variegated faces of its landscape—shady forests, glass-still lakes, emerald green

pastures, golden fields—Umbria's culinary traditions are also multi-facetted. One example is the contrast between the typically simple, but full of flavor dishes developed by Umbria's largely peasant population, and the rich, complex, beguiling flavors of the chocolates produced in the Umbrian city of Perugia. Perugia is synonymous with chocolate and produces some of the finest in the world. Tens of thousands of chocolate lovers from around the globe come to the city's annual Eurochocolate Festival to revel in tastings, exhibits, readings, and plays that commemorate this "food of the gods." From decadent chocolate cakes and torts, to hand-pressed coffees and liqueurs laced with chocolate, to the delicious chunks of chocolate itself, this is an event to savor for even the most avid chocolate lover's cravings—temporarily, at least.

Mousse di Gianduia

chocolate and toasted hazelnut mousse

SERVES 6

7 ounces dark chocolate
2 ounces peeled hazelnuts
3 tablespoons sugar
4 eggs, separated
4 cups heavy cream
Pinch of salt

Break the chocolate into small pieces and then place in a saucepan over medium heat. Allow the chocolate to slowly melt and remove from heat.

Toast the hazelnuts in the oven and set aside.

When cool, dice the hazelnuts (reserving about 2 teaspoons for garnish) and toss with the sugar and egg yolks. When combined, add to the melted chocolate and stir well; set aside.

Whisk the cream into stiff peaks and set half aside. Slowly add the other half to the chocolate mixture.

Whisk the egg whites with the salt until they are stiff; add to the chocolate cream mixture.

Pour the chocolate cream mixture into small bowls and refrigerate for at least 2 hours.

Before serving, top with the remaining cream and sprinkle with remaining toasted hazelnuts.

LIQUORE AL CIOCCOLATO

chocolate liqueur

SERVES 4

9 ounces high-quality bitter cocoa powder
4 cups sugar
1 vanilla bean
3 cups whole milk
1 cup Everclear (or similar grain alcohol)

In a saucepan over medium heat, add the cocoa powder, sugar, vanilla bean, and milk; bring to a boil, but do not scald. Immediately remove from heat and let cool.

When cool, remove the vanilla bean and add the alcohol. Stir well and refrigerate at least 24 hours before serving.

True, genuine chocolate—an essential ingredient in many Italian desserts—

is made from the fermented, roasted, and ground beans taken from the pod of the cacao tree

DESSERT FESTIVAL, CAMPANIA

A FESTIVAL CALLED "Feast of Homemade Desserts" might conjure up images of apple pies, berry crisps, and perhaps a rice pudding or two. But for many Italians, the best restaurant in even the most cosmopolitan city is not some Michelin-starred dining extravaganza, but rather their nonna's, or grandmother's, home kitchen. So, don't expect only the standard favorites at Campania's Feast of Homemade Desserts; visitors will encounter a seemingly endless parade of sweets from simple to complex to indescribable. Discover biscottis of all kinds, tiramisu, tortoni, cannoli, zeppole, zabaglione, cakes, and fruit desserts; taste specialties like *sfogliatelle* (shell-shaped puff pastry filled with ricotta cheese), *baba* (soft leavened dough soaked in orange water and rum), and *scui* (little cream-filled pastries drenched in caramel) and be sure to save room for the tables laden with chocolate and almond-based cakes. With such a diverse range of sweet delights, one might expect that Italian home cooks have been developing these concoctions for centuries. But it wasn't until the rise of the middle class in the nineteenth-century, coupled with the increased availability and lower price of sugar, that sweets became more than a privilege of the aristocracy and a rare holiday treat. Once in the hands of everyday Italian cooks, however, the development and popularity of desserts spread as quickly as a cannoli disappeared from nonna's kitchen.

BISCOTTI ALLE MANDORE
anise almond biscotti

MAKES 24

3 large eggs
1 cup sugar
1 teaspoon salt
1 teaspoon vanilla extract
1/2 teaspoon anise extract
3 cups pastry flour
2 teaspoons baking powder
1 teaspoon anise seeds, crushed
1 cup whole almonds, roughly chopped

Preheat oven to 325 degrees F.

In a stand mixer with a whisk attachment, whip eggs, sugar, and salt on high, until thick and pale yellow, about 5 minutes.

Turn mixer to low and add extracts, flour, and baking powder that have been sifted together, then anise seeds and almonds. Don't over mix dough otherwise it will become too thin. To safeguard against this, stir by hand toward the end if needed.

Form dough into a 3 x 16-inch-long log and place on a baking sheet. Press down to flatten top and bake about 60 minutes. Remove pan from oven and let cool, about 10 minutes. Turn oven down to 300 degrees F.

Cut biscotti into 1/2-inch-wide slices and place back on baking sheet. Bake 10 minutes and then turn over and cook 10 minutes more.

GRATIN DI FRUTTI DI BOSCO AL ZABAGLIONE

zabaglione gratin

SERVES 8

Assorted fresh fruits (strawberries, blueberries, raspberries, peaches, pears, plums, apricots or kiwi), or a single fruit, cleaned, peeled and sliced as needed to place in gratin dishes
5 egg yolks
1/2 cup sugar
1/2 cup Marsala wine
Powdered sugar

Preheat broiler or use a torch to brûlée.

Place desired fruit into eight individual gratin dishes, keeping fruit below the rim; set aside.

Fill a medium saucepan one-fourth full of water and bring to a simmer. Use a stainless steel bowl large enough to set over water. Add egg yolks and sugar to bowl and whisk thoroughly.

Set over the simmering water and whisk constantly, until it starts to thicken. Add wine and continue to whisk until doubled in volume, becoming thick and pale; remove from heat occasionally if it seems too hot.

Pour hot zabaglione over fruit dishes. Sprinkle with powdered sugar and brûlée till golden brown and serve.

Some of Italy's food festivals showcase the "love of desserts" **as their central theme.**

LEMON FESTIVAL, CAMPANIA

IMAGINE ACRE AFTER ACRE of lemon trees planted along Campania's sunny coastline, their floral and citrus aromas mingling with the fresh, salty tang of the sea breezes. Ready to go? While Campania is justly famous for its handcrafted pasta, traditional biscuits, and mozzarella cheeses, the enchanting towns of Procida and Sorrento are most celebrated for their spectacular lemons. Every year in early summer, the region's Lemon Festival displays these golden treasures, including the noted *Massa Lubrense* lemon. But the focal point of the show for many is the one-of-a-kind liqueur made from these lemons: Limoncello. This world-famous lemon liqueur is concocted from fresh lemon rinds, clear grain alcohol, water, and sugar, producing a bright yellow liqueur that is sweet and lemony but never sour, since it contains no lemon juice. Other favorite ways for festival-goers to stay cool in the summer sun are lemon ice cream, lemon *granita* (ice), and crisp, cool caprese salads infused with fresh lemon.

FRITTELLE DI RICOTTA AL LIMONE
lemon ricotta fritter

MAKES 1 DOZEN

8 ounces ricotta
¹/₄ cup sugar
Pinch of salt
Zest of 1 lemon
2 yolks
¹/₂ cup all-purpose flour
2 teaspoons baking powder
1 quart oil
Powdered sugar

In a medium bowl, add ricotta, sugar, salt, and zest. Mix well to remove lumps then add yolks. Sift flour and baking powder over mixture and stir to blend; cover and let batter rest 1 hour.

In a heavy skillet, heat oil. Using a thermometer, bring to a temperature of 350 degrees F.

Use a small ice cream scoop to spoon batter into oil. Fry 3 to 4 minutes, turning once until deep golden brown. Remove with a slotted spoon and transfer to a paper towel–lined plate.

Dust with powdered sugar and serve.

Sorbetto al Limone
lemon sorbet in lemon shells

SERVES 8

10 lemons, 2 reserved for juicing and zest
1½ cups sugar
2 cups water

Cut 1-inch off the top of 8 lemons, reserving cap for finished presentation. Make a shallow slice off the bottom of the same lemons, being careful not to cut through to the inside of the lemon, so that the lemon won't tip over (optional).

Carve out the insides of the lemons, reserving juice and flesh. Press the lemon flesh through a sieve to extract as much lemon juice as possible. Measure out 1 1/4 cups juice. If needed, use the reserved lemons for juice. Zest those lemons first before juicing and reserve the zest.

Place hollowed out lemon shells in a gallon freezer bag and freeze 1 hour or overnight.

Make syrup by adding the sugar and water to a saucepan; stir and bring to a boil. Add lemon zest and let simmer 5 minutes; set aside to cool. Remove from heat, add lemon juice, cool and strain through a fine sieve. Cover and refrigerate several hours until thoroughly chilled.

Process lemon mixture in an ice cream-sorbet maker, according to manufacturer's instructions.

Fill the frozen lemon shells with sorbet, and place in freezer at least 1 hour or overnight.

PISTACHIO FESTIVAL, SICILIA

SICILY'S YEARLY PISTACHIO FESTIVAL is about more than eating this green culinary gem. The local pistachio growers open their farms to guided tours and, since the festival is held at the height of the Sicilian pistachio harvest, everything from picking to packaging is on view. Plus, of course, just-picked pistachios are available for sampling. During this tasty event, many other Sicilian products are displayed at stands and simple tables speckling the roadsides throughout the Etna area. But the headliner is the pistachio in all its permutations and preparations. Visitors to the festival sample an array of pistachio dishes while learning yet more interesting facts about the delectable little nut. For instance, the shells of commercially available pistachios used to be dyed red or green. Why? To hide stains on the shells caused when the nuts were picked by hand. Today, most pistachios are picked by machine, and now the shells are left in their beautiful light beige color.

GELATO DI PISTACCHIO
pistachio gelato

SERVES 6–8

4 cups whole milk, divided
1 cup sugar
3 tablespoons cornstarch
2 cups shelled unsalted pistachios, finely ground in a food processor

In a medium saucepan over medium heat, bring 3 cups of the milk to a simmer; remove from heat.

Whisk together the remaining milk, sugar, and cornstarch and then whisk into hot milk. Return pan to heat and cook, stirring until mixture thickens, about 8 to 10 minutes.

In a large bowl, pour hot milk mixture over pistachios and then set aside to cool, stirring often; cover and refrigerate overnight.

Strain the mixture through a fine mesh strainer, pressing pistachios with a spoon. Discard the pistachios and continue to process in an ice cream maker according to the manufacturer's instruction.

PISTACCIO
€ 7,90

PRICKLY PEAR FESTIVAL, SICILIA

BETWEEN SICILY'S TALL mountains and its dramatic coastline, rolling hills and expansive flatlands abound. These areas between mountain and sea get quite dry in the summer; with the exception of the Plain of Catania at the foot of towering Mt. Etna, most of their rivers and streams have disappeared by July. This makes a perfect environment for the prickly pear—a nonnative cactus that is actually an American import. Sicilians have adopted this plant as their own, however, and celebrate its unique culinary possibilities with its own festival. For those unfamiliar, the edible part of prickly pears is the colorful oval-shaped fruits that emerge from the large green paddles of the cactus leaves. Like most cacti, the pear's juicy interior is protected by a tough, spine-studded outer skin. This outer skin must be removed (carefully!) before consumption; if not done properly, some of the tiny, nearly invisible spines may remain and be ingested, causing discomfort to the lips, tongue, and throat. But the luscious interior is well worth the effort, and visitors to the Prickly Pear Festival can sample the many creative ways Sicilians use it: in candies and jelly as a succulent accompaniment to desserts, or fermented into a delicious liqueur. The pear's gel-like liquid is also used as a natural conditioner.

SOUFFLÉ DI FICHI D'INDIA
prickly pear soufflé

SERVES 4

6 tablespoons sugar
3 egg yolks
2 tablespoons flour
1/2 cup skinned and diced prickly pear, puréed in a blender or food processor
6 egg whites, whipped to soft peaks
Butter for ramekins
Powdered sugar, as needed

Preheat oven to 350 degrees F.

In a bowl, mix the sugar, yolks, flour, and prickly pear. Fold in the egg whites. Divide the mixture into buttered ramekins and bake for about 20 to 25 minutes.

Serve with a sprinkle of powered sugar on top.

Zuccotto di Fichi d'India

prickly pear cake

SERVES 4

2 (10-ounce) fresh pound cakes
(or store-bought ladyfingers)
1/4 cup orange liqueur
1 cup heavy cream, whipped with
1/4 cup powdered sugar
1 pint strawberries, washed,
stemmed, and sliced
4 ripe prickly pears (green, orange, or
red), peeled and sliced 1/4 inch thick

Line a medium glass bowl with plastic wrap, allowing the wrap to hang over the top and sides.

Cut the pound cake into slices and strips. Tightly line the bowl with some of the cake pieces until the entire bottom and sides are covered.

With a brush, dab all of the pound cake with the orange liqueur.

Using a large spoon, add the whipped cream, then the strawberries, and prickly pear. Add a new layer of pound cake doused with orange liqueur and repeat the process with the whipped cream, strawberries, and prickly pear, creating layers until you have reached the top of the bowl.

Place a large plate on top of the bowl and flip the cake over, transferring the ingredients onto the plate.

Remove the plastic wrap and decorate the exterior with additional whipped cream, strawberries, and prickly pear. Refrigerate the cake for at least 2 hours before serving.

VARIATION: With a brush, glaze the exterior of the cake with 1/2 cup apricot jam.

STRAWBERRY FESTIVAL, VENETO

LIKE THE CHERRY, another famous fruit of Veneto is the strawberry. At the region's annual Strawberry Festival, not only the flavor but the colorful history of this luscious fruit is celebrated. For instance, did you know the Italian word for strawberry, *fragola,* comes from the word *fragans,* which means odorous, referring to the perfumed flesh of the fruit? Madame Tallien, an influential figure in the French Revolution, was nicknamed "Our Lady of Thermidor" for the strawberry baths she took to keep the radiant pink hue of her skin. Fontenelle, a centenarian writer and gourmet of the eighteenth century, attributed his long life to his steady diet of strawberries. In Argentina, in contrast, locals believed strawberries were poisonous until the mid-nineteenth century (much as Americans were originally convinced of the toxicity of tomatoes). At Veneto's Strawberry Festival, the prized fruit is showcased in scattered, colorful stands, the most popular of which are in the dessert section. Here, strawberry dishes from the simple to the extravagant present Italian strawberries at their finest.

FRAGOLE CON ACETO BALSAMICO
strawberries with balsamic vinegar and sugar

SERVES 6

2 pints fresh strawberries
1/2 cup sugar
3 tablespoons aged balsamic vinegar

Wash strawberries and remove the tops with a paring knife. Transfer strawberries to a serving bowl, and toss with the sugar until well coated.

Transfer the sugar-coated strawberries to a serving plate and drizzle with balsamic vinegar before serving.

CRESPELLE DI FRAGOLE

strawberry crepes with strawberry and port wine sauce

SERVES 4

2/3 cup flour

3 eggs

1/3 cup sugar

1 cup milk

4 tablespoons butter, melted and divided

Pinch of salt

1 pound fresh strawberries, washed and stemmed

1/2 cup port wine

1/4 cup powdered sugar

In a mixer, blend the flour, eggs, sugar, milk, 3 tablespoons butter, and salt. Remove from mixer and let rest for 40 minutes.

Using a 10-inch nonstick pan with remaining butter, pour in 1/4 cup of the crepe mixture and cook until lightly golden on each side. Repeat until all the mixture is used. Transfer the crepes to a dish and keep warm until ready to serve.

In a mixer, add half of the strawberries, port wine, and half of the powdered sugar; blend well.

In a separate bowl, add the strawberry mixture. Cut the remaining strawberries in half and add to mixture.

Pour a ladle of strawberry mixture on each crepe and roll to seal in the berries.

Top each crepe with a scoop of the strawberry mixture and remaining powdered sugar.

At Veneto's Strawberry Festival, the delicious fruit

is enjoyed fresh off the vine or blended in refreshing gelatos.

STRUDEL, MUSCAT WINE, AND VIN SANTO WINE FESTIVAL, TRENTINO ALTO ADIGE

THROUGHOUT THE NORTHERN REGION of Trentino, more than one hundred villages and towns host some kind of market, fair, or festival—adding yet more reasons this mountainous region is a popular tourist destination. The Spring Fair, for example, draws over 100,000 visitors to sample the locally made foods and browse among the arts, crafts, and distinct products of the region. Because Trentino's cuisine tends toward hearty fare often followed with a light dessert of fresh fruit from the region's abundant cherry, plum, and apple trees, fruit and dessert festivals are prominent among the area's many activities. During the Strudel, Muscat Wine and Vin Santo Wine Festival, these well-appreciated pairings are proffered in the many cafes, bars, pastry shops, and bakeries throughout Trentino. Although the popularity of apple strudel shows the regional influence of neighboring Austria and Switzerland, the cooks of Trentino have transformed it into a traditional Italian dessert that draws pastry lovers from all across the country.

STRUDEL DI MELE
apple strudel

SERVES 4

¹/₂ cup butter
1 package frozen puff pastry dough, thawed
2 pounds fresh apples, peeled and sliced
Rind of 1 lemon
¹/₄ cup raisins
3 tablespoons pine nuts
2 teaspoons cinnamon
¹/₄ cup sugar
1 egg, beaten

GARNISH
Powdered sugar, for garnish

Preheat oven to 375 degrees F.

Melt the butter and then brush over the thawed puff pastry dough.

In a mixing bowl, combine the apple slices with the lemon rind and then add the raisins and pine nuts. Add the cinnamon and sugar and toss well.

Lay out the pastry dough on the kitchen counter and spread the apple mixture evenly over the dough. Then with your fingers, roll the dough, keeping the apple mixture tightly inside.

Place the rolled dough on a baking sheet and brush the outside of the pastry with the egg. Bake the roll for about 1 hour.

Sprinkle the finished strudel with powdered sugar before serving.

WATERMELON FESTIVAL, CAMPANIA

WHAT BETTER WAY to cool off on a hot summer day than at a festival dedicated to a fruit whose very name promises refreshment? The fruit is watermelon, the time is August, and the setting is beautiful Campania. Like its luscious lemons, Campania's watermelons merit a festival all their own. Here, visitors can drink watermelon in summer cocktails, feast on grilled watermelon steak (aptly named because it resembles a seared beef steak), and nibble on watermelon rinds that have been stir-fried, stewed, or pickled. Even the seeds are part of the show: rich in fat and protein, the seeds are toasted and eaten as a snack, added to other dishes, and pressed for their oil. But the Watermelon Festival isn't all about eating: watermelons turn into rolling speedsters in the popular Watermelon Race, as both visitors and locals cheer their favorite melons across the finish line.

MACEDONIA D'ARANCIA ROSSA
melon balls in blood orange sauce

SERVES 8

MELON BALLS
1 small sweet seedless watermelon
1 small sweet seeded cantaloupe

SAUCE
1 cup sugar
1 cup fresh blood orange-lemon juice
(about 3 oranges & 1 lemon)

Scoop out melons with a melon baller and place in a medium bowl.

Combine sauce in a small saucepan over medium-high heat until boiling. Turn down heat to simmer and continue until reduced to 1 cup, about 15 minutes. Let cool to room temperature, then pour over fruit and refrigerate until serving.

GRANITA DI COCOMERO
watermelon granita

SERVES 8

4 to 5 cups packed watermelon
1 cup sugar
1 cup water
Juice of 1 lemon

Purée watermelon in a blender until smooth and then strain through a fine mesh strainer.

Stir together sugar and water in a saucepan over high heat. Bring to a simmer and then remove from heat. Add the sugar syrup and lemon juice to the watermelon purée and stir well. Pour into a 9 x 13-inch glass or metal pan and transfer to the freezer uncovered.

Using the tines of a fork, stir mixture thoroughly to break up ice every 30 minutes, for about 4 hours, or until granita is slushy and frozen.

Serve in individual chilled glasses or freeze up to 4 days.

During Italy's hot summer days, watermelon is the favorite fruit among locals

ACKNOWLEDGMENTS

Chef Leonardo Curti and author James O. Fraioli would like to personally thank the following individuals for their generous support and assistance with this book:

Gibbs Smith, Melissa Barlow, and the entire editorial staff at Gibbs Smith; Andrea Hurst and Andrea Hurst Literary Management; designer Debra McQuiston; photographers Brian Hodges, Luca Trovato, and James J. Fraioli; food and prop stylist Rori Trovato; Pompilio Fabrizi and Emanuela Boni of the Italian Government Tourist Board; Trattoria Grappolo and the community of Santa Ynez Valley; Alfonso and Giorgio Curti; Jennifer, Sophia, Isabella, and Camilla Curti; Luigi Antonio Curti and Maria Santoro; Linda Vathayanon; Cindy Fraioli; Rachelle and Tish; Jim, Karin, and Tanya Fraioli; and all the participating Italian food festivals, which were a pleasure to visit.

PHOTO CREDITS

Food photography provided by Luca Trovato
Festival food photography provided by Brian Hodges
Additional festival photography provided by Brian Hodges and James J. Fraioli
Additional photography provided by: The Italian Government Tourist Board North America-Fototeca Enit, and Ente Turismo Alba Bra Langhe Roero.

Metric Conversion Chart

Liquid and Dry Measures

U.S.	Canadian	Australian
¼ teaspoon	1 mL	1 ml
½ teaspoon	2 mL	2 ml
1 teaspoon	5 mL	5 ml
1 tablespoon	15 mL	20 ml
¼ cup	50 mL	60 ml
⅓ cup	75 mL	80 ml
½ cup	125 mL	125 ml
⅔ cup	150 mL	170 ml
¾ cup	175 mL	190 ml
1 cup	250 mL	250 ml
1 quart	1 liter	1 litre

Temperature Conversion Chart

Fahrenheit	Celsius
250	120
275	140
300	150
325	160
350	180
375	190
400	200
425	220
450	230
475	240
500	260